TREK: DEEP SPACE NINE

THE UNAUTHORIZED STORY

JAMES VAN HISE

Library of Congress Cataloging-in-Publication Data
James Van Hise

Trek: Deep Space Nine The Unauthorized Story

1. Trek: Deep Space Nine The Unauthorized Story (television, popular culture)
I. Title

Published by Pioneer Books, Inc., 5715 N. Balsam Rd., Las Vegas, NV, 89130.

First Printing, 1993

DEDICATION

TO

GENE RODDENBERRY

Who Started It All

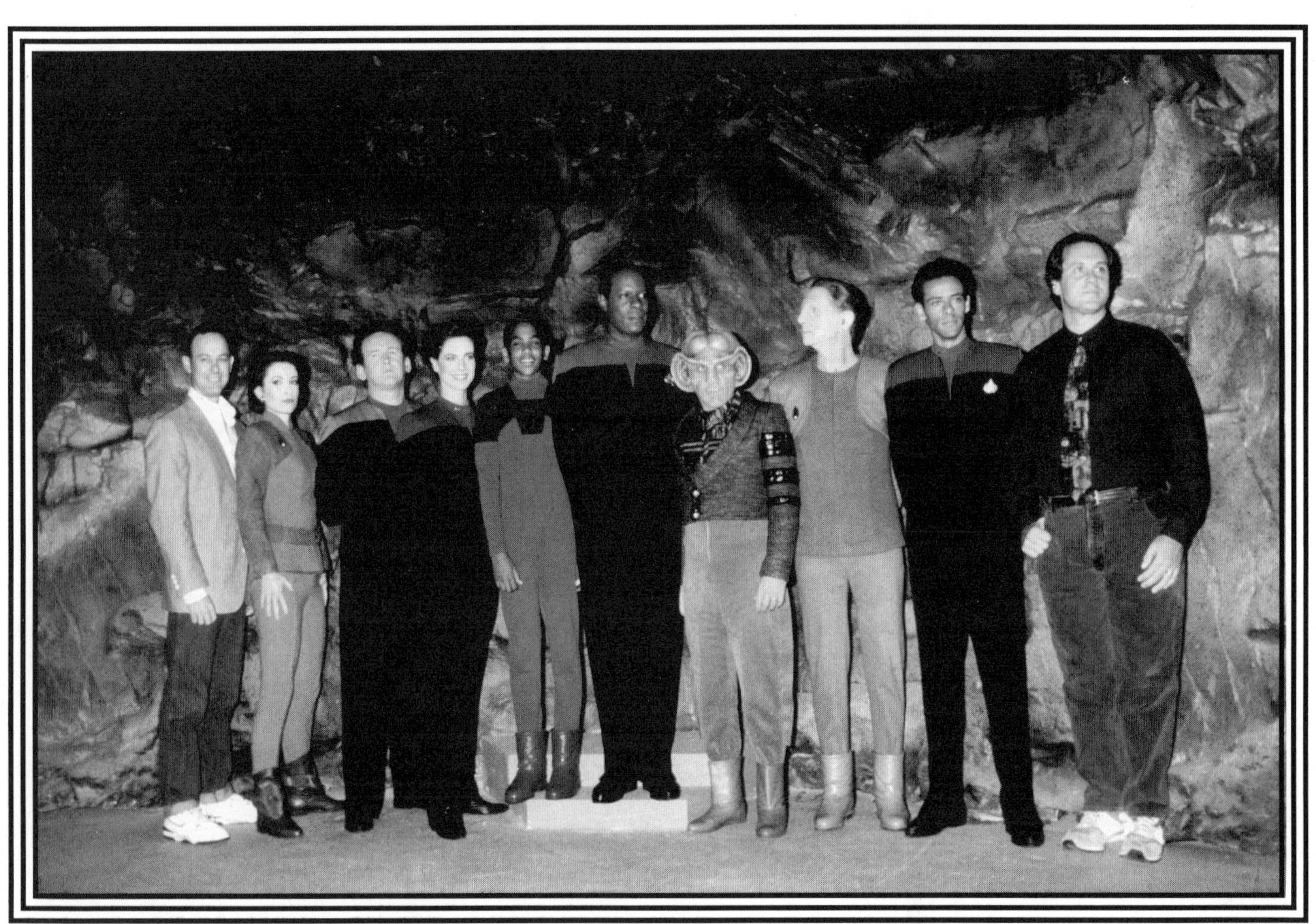

The cast from DEEP SPACE NINE.

TREK: DEEP SPACE NINE

THE UNAUTHORIZED STORY

On September 2, 1992 the cast of DEEP SPACE NINE was presented to the public for the first time at a special press conference held at Paramount Studios. Pictured here from the left are Colm Meaney, Terry Farrell, Cirroc Lofton, Avery Brooks, Armin Shimerman and Rene Auberjonois.

Photo: ©1993 Ortega/Ron Galella Ltd.

One good spin-off deserves another. While STAR TREK: THE NEXT GENERATION got off to an uneasy start in 1987, it soon found its wings and has been at or near the top of the syndicated ratings ever since. It was only a question of when Paramount would decide to try to catch lightning in a bottle for the third time for now they had the confidence of repeated success behind them and the people on staff with the proven know-how to do it.

INTRODUCTION
TREK: THE THIRD GENERATION

DEEP SPACE NINE features several regular characters. The commander of the space station is Benjamin Sisko, a Starfleet captain who was serving with his wife, Jennifer, on board one of the vessels attacked by Picard when the Enterprise Captain had been transformed into Locutus of Borg. The man's wife was killed in the attack and he had been rotated back to Earth in semi-retirement to recover from the ordeal. His command of the space station is his first active duty post since his wife was killed three years before. He finds it difficult to accept that Picard was *completely* helpless to stop the attack. But Sisko's feelings about Picard were completely resolved in the premiere episode, "Emissary," thereby resolving that conflict immediately rather than continuing it into the series. Along with Sisko on Deep Space Nine is his son, Jake, played by Cirroc Lofton.

"We felt that a father and son relationship would be a different relationship than any other STAR TREK kind of hero that we've seen before," series co-creator Michael Piller explains. "He has found himself at a place in his life that he can't quite get beyond and he's sent to this space station, and he really doesn't like this assignment because this space station was built by the Cardassians who have just abandoned it. The Bajorans are struggling with the potential of civil war." Piller's description of the Bajorans has proven to be somewhat exaggerated as thus far the planet Bajor has been talked about a lot more than it's been visited and seen, and the people there might just as well be a million miles away for all the impact they've had on story lines.

Although Sisko wasn't initially happy with his assignment, all this changed when the stable wormhole was discovered. The importance of Deep Space Nine became elevated immeasurably in the eyes of the Federation. In further describing this character, Piller said, "He is sent on a quest and in this whole pilot episode it is a personal quest for this man who has lost his way and

must conquer the dragon, but in this case he must conquer his personal dragons in order to move on with his life and to grow as a man and to be a good father and to be a good officer. And so what we will find in this show is a man who is coming to Deep Space Nine, but is coming to find himself." But thus far is seems that Sisko found himself in the premiere episode as that marked the only personal drama the character has experienced to date. Even when Dax, his old friend, was threatened, she refused to confide in him, thus diluting the possible dramatic conflict by making it remote.

AN ALIEN FOR ANY OCCASION

Another character is a shapeshifter, Odo, who is also the security chief. Odo came from a world on the other side of the wormhole, but he does not remember his past, having been found aboard a drifting spacecraft fifty years before. In order to fit in among the people who found him, he has chosen to adopt a humanoid form, but his efforts at maintaining this form are imperfect. The producers have states that this character will be used to explore the nature of humanity and what truly defines one as being human. In this way he will occupy the position of Spock and Data as those characters have been used to act as a mirror of humanity in the other two STAR TREK series. But being neither part human nor an android, the approach will be completely different from that taken with either Spock or Data.

Odo is played by Rene Auberjonois and is already being touted as one of the main characters to emerge from the series. "He is the curmudgeon of all curmudgeons," Piller states. "So instead of Data who worships humanity and wants to be that, and Spock who would deny it, Odo has been forced to pass as a humanoid all of his life, to look like us and act like us because it's a lot more socially acceptable and he resents it. So he has now found a way to use it as a defense mechanism and keep a distance from it and find ways to be critical of the human condition." "He is one of a kind," Piller revealed. "He was found near where this wormhole shows up, as an infant in a spacecraft, which we are going to assume probably came out of the Gamma Quadrant. But he has no idea where he came from and he's always searching for his identity."

Regarding the make-up which disguises him, the actor explained, "It's a mask but it feels what I feel is in the script for the character, and I find it very evocative." One plot thread which has been revealed regarding Odo is that Majel Barrett will appear at some point as Lwaxana Troi and will become a romantic interest for the alien shape shifter. When he reveals to her that he has to turn into a bucket of liquid every night, she unhesitatingly replies, "That's okay. I can swim."

Odo had emerged from the wormhole fifty years before and had served the Cardassians on the space station long before Starfleet determined that Deep Space Nine had any strategic importance. The alien is just as willing to assist Starfleet as he did the Cardassians for the past half century. With Starfleet planning to explore the galaxy through the wormhole, he believes that he may at last uncover the clues he needs to unlock the secrets to his past. A shape shifter similar to this alien appeared in STAR TREK VI—THE UNDISCOVERED COUNTRY.

TROUBLE-SHOOTER

Colm Meaney, whose role as Miles O'Brien, the Transporter Chief, had been growing on THE NEXT GENERATION, was transferred from the Enterprise in the premiere episode of DEEP SPACE NINE where he became Chief of Operations on the station. His character changes are explored as the viewers compare his Enterprise duties with his duties on Deep Space Nine.

"We've always thought he was a terrific performer," Piller states, "and now we're giving him something much more interesting to do as a leading character on the new show. He is pulling his hair out from one minute to the next because everything is breaking down. He can't get the replicators to make a good cup of coffee; his wife Keiko is terribly unhappy about having been taken off the Enterprise and over to this dreadful space station. So he finds himself in an uncomfortable position." The subplot with Keiko was resolved early on when she opened a school for the children living on the station, and in fact her character has largely been relegated to the back ground ever since.

The science officer aboard the space station is played by Terry Farrell. Lt. Jadzia Dax is an alien known as a Trill. The Trill were introduced in the NEXT GENERATION episode "The Host," where we were shown that the Trill are a dual species that join to become a single entity. Since the sex of the host body is unimportant to the Trill, the three hundred year old Dax now inhabits the body of a young woman. Previously Dax inhabited the body of an older man, Curzon Dax, who was a mentor of Captain Benjamin Sisko's. But in its new body, Sisko finds that he's physically attracted to Dax.

Originally they had conceived Dax as being a very serene and focused character, but according to Piller, "The more we've written her, the more we're finding that she is not what she appears to be. That underneath this placid exterior, there's all these various personalities that she's gone through that are in turmoil and there's a lot of inner conflict. You know all the voices we hear inside of ourselves are all made up of different subpersonalities; well she's got them all screaming at her in a variety of different ways."

A DOCTOR AND A QUARK

Siddig El Fadil plays Dr. Julian Bashir, a twenty-seven year old Starfleet medical officer. His youth and inexperience will be emphasized since he has just graduated from Starfleet Medical and this is his first post outside of the Sol system. Dr. Bashir thinks he knows it all and has a knack for rubbing people the wrong way, although he means well and is a very likable character. Piller speaks highly of the actor, stating, "He's able to take this character, who can be very grating on the nerves, and make him charming."

Armin Shimerman plays the Ferengi bartender, Quark. Quark is one of the shifty, untrustworthy aliens introduced in year one of THE NEXT GENERATION. He has his hands into all sorts of illegal and improper activities going on behind the scenes aboard Deep Space Nine. His ongoing presence is intended to create constant conflicts aboard the space station, but as a series regular he'll be in a position to have a more fully developed role than any Ferengi who has been presented to date. In fact he will forge a friendship of a sort with Benjamin Sisko, and will be liked (but not entirely trusted) by his compatriots. The actor explains that, like THE NEXT GENERATION, in DEEP SPACE NINE the staff has created, "fascinating aliens that have three sides." One of the more interesting relationships on the show is that between Quark and Odo, as they're sworn enemies who have an on-going verbal conflict. Before the series aired, those involved with the show were predicting that Quark would emerge as the most popular character. The fact that he has been thus far written and portrayed as pretty much of a cartoon rather than a character has tended to limit that possibility a great deal.

DEEP SPACE NINE is not noticeably different from THE NEXT GENERATION in style and approach. And like any new series, is suffering from growing pains. The characters, who seemed so clearly defined in "Emissary," have become subservient to the plots. Major Kira, who was clearly antagonistic to Commander Sisko initially, is suddenly completely accepting of him and the Federation presence. In fact she seems no less a Federation representative than is Sisko himself. Only the character of Odo has managed to keep from being brushed into blandness by the writing, and this may owe more to the actor who has much more experience than anyone else on the series and is bringing all of that experience to bear to keep from becoming just a colorful prop for the storylines.

UNFRIENDLY ALIENS

The Cardassians form the continuing threat in the series as the space station is right on the edge of Cardassian space. The Bajoran home world, which is the planet which Deep Space Nine is in orbit around, was ravaged by the Cardassians before they left it as they were overthrown by the Bajorans in a civil war. This left the Bajorans in a sorry state as the planet had been so severely damaged in the war that the Bajorans were left with nothing to rebuild with. This is why the Bajorans have turned to the Federation and requested admission, although many of them continue to resent the fact that the Federation maintained a neutral distance while the Bajoran people were being exploited and brutalized by the Cardassians.

The presence of warring cultures was also key to the basis of the series. "Our whole goal was to create more conflict everywhere you turn in this series. So what you have as a result are people who have different agendas. You've got Major Kira, who is a Bajoran, who really doesn't want the Federation to be there, and as a result she and Sisko are in conflict. You've got Odo and Quark who are in conflict. You've got Sisko and Quark who are in conflict. Everywhere you turn you've got conflict in the show. But what we found as a result of that is not only good drama, but a lot more humor than we expected to have."

While humor is always a good idea when kept in balance, it has largely replaced the initial conflict presented in the series premiere. Odo and Quark have a humorous conflict rather than a dramatic one, just as Sisko does with Quark. In "The Passenger," even though Quark is shown providing hired mercenaries at the behest of a brutal murderer, he's portrayed almost as though he is being forced to do it. The humorous chicanery of Quark ceases being funny in this episode and yet the story takes a distinctly neutral stand on whether what Quark did was wrong. There is no confrontation with the Ferengi even though those mercenaries hijack a spacecraft and threaten the safety of Deep Space Nine itself.

Berman and Piller had been pushing for a spin-off from THE NEXT GENERATION for two years, and when they worked out the details of DEEP SPACE NINE, Paramount was quite enthusiastic in their support of the series concept and gave the producers a great deal of latitude in the casting. Michael Piller states that, "There is absolutely no truth to the rumor that the arrival of DEEP SPACE NINE is the end of THE NEXT GENERATION. THE NEXT GENERATION is continuing." How long it is continuing remains to be seen. Majel Barrett was once quoted as stating that THE NEXT GENERATION was projected to run for six seasons, whereupon the syndication package would be considered complete. But indications are strong that the series will have at least a seventh season.

THE REJECTED INVITATION

DEEP SPACE NINE is set aboard a space station in orbit around the planet Bajor. The space station was being used by the Cardassians to exploit the mining resources of the Bajoran home world. When the Bajorans finally overthrew the despotic rule of the Cardassians, the Federation placed personnel aboard Deep Space Nine to oversee its operation and make sure everything stays cordial and cooperative. But while the

Federation personnel will not be officially acting as police, their presence is consciously there to discourage the Cardassians from trying to bother the newly liberated Bajorans. Since the Bajorans have applied for membership in the Federation, their presence there is by the invitation of Bajor.

The Bajorans have been previously encountered as they are the race to which Ensign Ro belongs. While Ensign Ro is an ex-terrorist who was more-or-less drafted into Starfleet due to her expertise in certain matters, DEEP SPACE NINE will deal with a different aspect of the Bajorans. While the character of Ensign Ro was initially announced as appearing in this new series, the actress, Michelle Forbes, chose to bow out to pursue other projects, while remaining as an occasional character on THE NEXT GENERATION.

THE FUTURE OF STAR TREK

The stories, many of which are confined to the station, create a claustrophobic sensation on the show. This has caused rather confining situations on the plots as well. It wasn't until episode eleven, "Vortex," that we finally got out and about again like we did in "The Emissary," as Odo went through the wormhole and into the Gamma Quadrant. Granted, all we saw was a rocky asteroid but there was also a space battle which in some respects was a reprise of the one seen eleven years ago in STAR TREK II—THE WRATH OF KHAN. Now if only we could visit those mysterious archaeological sites referred to in "Q Less" we might finally see some real otherworld excitement.

Set in the year 2360 A.D., the new series is contemporary with THE NEXT GENERATION. While the extent of cross-overs between the two series have yet to be fully determined. STAR TREK: DEEP SPACE NINE was launched with a two hour premiere, "Emissary," which included a stopover from the Enterprise and Jean-Luc Picard. But Starfleet personnel accustomed to the clean, modern conveniences of starship life find very different things to contend with aboard the space station. These include a casino and a holographic brothel as the station also serves as a port of call for merchant ships. But once the station was cleaned up in early episodes, any "darker" aspects to the show all but vanished.

A crossover between DEEP SPACE NINE and THE NEXT GENERATION took place in March 1993 in the two part TNG episode "Birthright." Worf stops over on Deep Space Nine and encounters someone who claims to know where his long lost Klingon father is. The station actually plays just a peripheral element in the storyline as the DEEP SPACE NINE regulars are not involved in the drama or the action which follows.

By establishing DEEP SPACE NINE as being contemporary with THE NEXT GENERATION, characters from that series could still turn up on the new series even after TNG goes off the air. With the highly rated appearance of

James Doohan on THE NEXT GENERATION in the fall of 1992, Doohan has reportedly been urging Paramount to add him to the cast of DEEP SPACE NINE. Less certain are rumors wherein Shatner has expressed interest in participating in DEEP SPACE NINE in some respect, which would be a surprise since he has steadfastly refused to be involved in THE NEXT GENERATION (which has thus far been visited by Dr. McCoy, Mr. Spock and Montgomery Scott) and in fact Shatner claims never to have watched the show.

THE NEXT GENERATION is slated to go into production as a new series of feature films once the seventh season runs out. No doubt such a feature film would also include some sort of crossover from DEEP SPACE NINE.

It's hard to believe that back in the 70's, many people were saying that STAR TREK was just old news and that nothing would ever be done with the premise again. DEEP SPACE NINE has shown that there are many more directions in which that concept created by Gene Roddenberry and company can be spun, and the success of DEEP SPACE NINE will no doubt lead to even more spin-offs in the years to come.

The full cast of DEEP SPACE NINE. From left, Nana Visitor, Colm Meaney, Terry Farrell, Cirroc Lofton, Avery Brooks, Armin Shimerman, and Rene Auberjonois.

Photo ©1993 Ortega. Ron Galella Ltd.

When Paramount announced the launch of THE NEXT GENERATION almost seven years ago, there were more doubters than believers. Following its unqualified success, it was inevitable that they'd return to Roddenberry's realm for yet another run at the stars.

BEHIND THE SCENES: THE CREATION

January 1993 marked the deep space launch of STAR TREK: DEEP SPACE NINE. Ironically the announcement of the plans to produce this series came shortly after the death of Gene Roddenberry in late 1991. The timing led to speculation that had Roddenberry lived, this series might not have. Suspicions along these lines were raised particularly after descriptions of this new series filtered out. "It's going to be darker and grittier than THE NEXT GENERATION," executive producer Rick Berman stated in the March 6, 1992 ENTERTAINMENT WEEKLY. "The characters won't be squeaky clean."

To the fans, STAR TREK has always meant just that—squeaky clean heroes. What would Gene Roddenberry have thought of this? After all, people close to him have stated that Gene hated STAR TREK VI merely because it postulated Enterprise crew members who were anti-Klingon bigots. In the future that Roddenberry made, humankind had outgrown such pettiness. Gene overlooked the fact that in the 1966 STAR TREK episode "Balance of Terror," an Enterprise crewman was postulated as being an angry anti-Romulan bigot who transferred his feelings of mistrust and suspicion to Mr. Spock when it was discovered that Romulans and Vulcans were of the same race. As it has turned out, though, the only character on the new series who has a real dark side is Quark. Major Kira is a former terrorist, but she fought on the correct side of the conflict. At worst, Dax had an affair with a married woman when the Trill was in her former host body, that of the man Curzon Dax. The characters couldn't be much more well-scrubbed than this.

Rick Berman and Michael Piller were originally at a loss for a title for the newest addition to the STAR TREK canon. They toyed with calling the series "The Final Frontier" and having the space station re-christened with a Starbase number after the Federation took over the day-to-day operations of the station. Having a series with a Cardassian or Bajoran name was not considered a terribly good marketing ploy. In the course of the series' development, the station was dubbed "Deep Space Nine," a temporary appellation which not only became permanent but which also became the title for the fledgling series itself, despite Piller and Berman's dissatisfaction with the name.

Even though the announcement about DEEP SPACE NINE seemed to come from out of nowhere several weeks after Roddenberry's death, Michael Piller and Rick Berman had actually been discussing ideas for a new series for some time. It was always planned to be a spin-off from STAR TREK. Even though the ideas were discussed with Paramount, it never went beyond the planning stages. When Brandon Tarticoff moved from being the head of NBC to being the head of Paramount, he told Rick Berman that he wanted to see a spin-off from STAR TREK to launch into syndication. Berman and Pillar returned to their series notes and worked up a proposal for DEEP SPACE NINE.

The reason that Paramount wanted a new STAR TREK television series to run concurrent with THE NEXT GENERATION is to help establish DEEP SPACE NINE so that when THE NEXT GENERATION goes into reruns, a new and different STAR TREK series will already have been established and be in place in the syndication market. STAR TREK: DEEP SPACE NINE is being syndicated with another new Paramount series, a revival of the fifties series THE UNTOUCHABLES. The ratings success of DEEP SPACE NINE, which has put it neck and neck with THE NEXT GENERATION, has thus far shown Paramount's judgment in launching the new series to be a sound one.

RODDENBERRY INFLUENCE

Rick Berman insists that DEEP SPACE NINE is not going to be his and executive producer Michael Piller's own personal take on STAR TREK. He states that this series is just another way of expressing Gene Roddenberry's vision and it is fitting and consistent with everything that has been done with STAR TREK before. DEEP SPACE NINE was initially announced as having been developed under Gene's guidance and with his input. However later statements contradicted this and indicated that while STAR TREK's creator was aware of the plans for DEEP SPACE NINE, he wasn't directly involved with it at any time.

Regarding Roddenberry's influence on DEEP SPACE NINE, Piller explained, "Every writer knows that we have a responsibility to maintain his vision. We take it very seriously. I got a letter from twenty-five grade school children, and the teacher, who said, 'Please, we use STAR TREK as an example of life in the future and the optimistic view and the hope that Gene gave us. We've heard that this is going to be dark and dreary.' And the truth is that it is not."

But by the time Roddenberry created the backdrop for THE NEXT GEN-

ERATION, he had adopted the philosophy that all the members of Starfleet should be in harmony, particularly those who work together on a starship. "He had very clear-cut rules about Starfleet officers having any tension or conflict between themselves. His futuristic humans were too good for that," Berman told VARIETY in the January 25, 1993 issue. "As a result, it's very difficult to write for these people, because out of conflict comes good drama."

THE DARK LIGHT YEARS?

Producer Rick Berman sees the show as a means of escaping the somewhat limiting constraints of Gene Roddenberry's original STAR TREK concept. "We set about creating a situation, an environment, and a group of characters that could have conflict without breaking Gene's rules. We took our characters and placed them in an unfamiliar environment, one that lacked the state-of-the-art comfort of the Enterprise, and where there were people who didn't want them there."

On Deep Space Nine, set in a rough and tumble corner of the known universe, Berman sees a lot more room for conflict. "By putting Starfleet characters on an alien space station with alien creatures, you have immediate conflicts.

"The truth is that there is more conflict," Pillar says, trying to put the show and its various elements into perspective, "that we're in a part of the universe that is giving us more conflict. And the fact that we are on an alien space station instead of the Enterprise will allow us to do that. But it is the same Gene Roddenberry optimism for the future of mankind that drives the vision of this show. There is not going to be any more shooting, more weapons or battles or anything like that. Certainly we're going to have action. It's going to be an adventure show and it's an entertainment show. We wanted to find the camaraderie that existed in the original STAR TREK, like that relationship between McCoy and Spock, and in order to do that you have to have differences, and differences between the characters on THE NEXT GENERATION are not so clearly defined."

One character whose personality is explored more is Miles O'Brien. He has more room to be curt and unpleasant from time to time. Less regimented than a Federation ship, the space station from which DEEP SPACE NINE draws its title, leaves its inhabitants more room to express the less agreeable aspects of their personalities from time to time. On the other hand, this also leads to scenes in which O'Brien and Commander Sisko discuss matters in a considerably more relaxed and informal fashion than O'Brien would ever have been able to employ while speaking with Captain Picard.

"There are characters who come through much darker than the NEXT GENERATION characters, but I don't know that I could say this is a dark series," Piller says reflectively. "It's still

Gene Roddenberry's vision. It has an optimistic view of mankind in the future. Reason and dialog and communication are still the key weapons in the fight to solve problems. I think the label of darker is probably exaggerated."

A NEW ORDER

Michael Piller never had any doubt that there was room for a third STAR TREK series. He feels that Gene Roddenberry created a huge universe of characters and concepts. "Gene used to say, somewhat in kidding, but in a way to communicate what he wanted to do with STAR TREK, that space was like the old west, and that STAR TREK was like WAGON TRAIN. In that whole genre of the west there were dozens of television shows. In the universe that Gene has created there is room, not only for a WAGON TRAIN, but also for a GUNSMOKE. In essence, what I think we're doing is the counterpart to the kind of shows you saw on the old west where you have a Ft. Sheridan on the edge of the frontier, and a frontier town in a very active area with a lot of people coming through it."

Among the other ideas Berman and Piller discussed was the concept of creating a sort of futuristic Hong Kong on a planet surface and building a set in the desert north of Los Angeles where they'd film the series.

"We felt that would be extremely expensive and difficult to produce," Piller stated in VARIETY, "so we took our Hong Kong and put it on a space station, then we scaled it back in order to make it cost-effective."

Berman explained that coming up with DEEP SPACE NINE after working on THE NEXT GENERATION was like living in a house for several years and then deciding to remodel.

"This was how we felt about STAR TREK. It was very close to us, but there was a lot of 'wouldn't it be nice.' Developing DEEP SPACE NINE gave us the opportunity to rebuild the house."

ORIGINS AND IDEAS

The groundwork for STAR TREK: DEEP SPACE NINE was created in a couple of episodes of THE NEXT GENERATION: "Ensign Ro" and "The Wounded." Viewers met their first Bajoran in the person of the troublesome Ensign Ro (portrayed by Michele Forbes), and got a glimpse of the difficult conditions on Bajor after a century of occupation by the genuinely disagreeable Cardassians. Just prior to the premiere of DEEP SPACE NINE, THE NEXT GENERATION featured a two-part episode in which Captain Picard was captured and tortured by Cardassians.

But it seems that much of what would lead to the ideas for DEEP SPACE NINE grew out of the political situation that was created for the fifth season NEXT GENERATION episode "Ensign Ro."

"We did not create Ensign Ro as a potential spin-off, but for all intents and purposes, that's where the tableau was set for this. We had intended to bring that character with us to DEEP SPACE NINE," Michael Piller explained on the QVC cable channel during his appearance there Dec. 5, 1992, "but the actress, who we love, Michelle Forbes, simply wasn't interested in doing a series. So after we had actually written a bible and created a script, we had to write that character out of it. But it all grew out of that character." A different actor, Nana Visitor, was cast in the role of the Bajoran regular on the series, Major Kira Nerys. She is Benjamin Sisko's first officer and the station's Bajoran attaché, and of her role she states, "The thing that is the most exciting is the script, and the fact that the women in the show are very strong, very powerful, and that it's a lot to do with what's going on in the world right now." Kira Nerys is portrayed as a strong action hero of the kind who would even lead rescue missions.

Berman and Piller wrote several different versions of the series bible while it was being developed. When they finally showed a later version to Paramount, the studio provided its own input into the project, and in fact Brandon Tarticoff (before he left Paramount) suggested that the show might be something like THE RIFLEMAN in outer space, although Berman and Piller didn't quite feel that this idea particularly fit in with what they were trying to develop. But the studio's suggestions were weighed and incorporated into the series concept to produce the final result used now. In fact the father and son idea that Brandon Tarticoff was talking about did appeal to Berman and Piller and that element is very much a part of the series. The series bible is called that because it serves as the basis of development for the entire series. All of the characters and their relationships are outlined in it as well as the background of everything used in the series.

The space station itself, often referred to simply as "DS9 ," was itself built by the Cardassians, to serve, among other things, as an orbiting watch tower over their unruly colony. When Commander Sisko finally comes to the station, however, he finds that it has been largely gutted by the departing imperialists.

BAJOR—A PLANET ABUSED

The space station, Deep Space Nine, was established by the Cardassians and the Bajorans in conjunction with other alien races. As a result it reflects cultural needs and biases often unfamiliar to some Starfleet personnel. The station was considered of remote interest until the first fixed, stationary wormhole was discovered near the star system where Bajor is located. In fact this wasn't discovered until after Commander Sisko was posted to the space station. This discovery, in fact, caused the Cardassians to consider retaking Deep Space Nine and Bajor for its strategic importance.

Bajor has been described as a stripped mining planet, but one whose culture is very conscious of the spiritual and the mystical. The Bajorans even believe that the stationary wormhole was created through divine intervention. Its existence has saved what was a dying, backwater world. One of the semi-regular characters is a religious leader from Bajor who holds very strong views on the purpose of the wormhole, although this aspect has not yet been played up. In fact the Kai has appeared only in "The Emissary" and has not had any important impact on the first ten episodes beyond that initial appearance. Named Kai Opaka, the series bible indicates that she is to be a semi-regular and provides a fairly adequate description of her. She is the spiritual leader of Bajor who is intended to provide a sharp counterpoint to the secular nature of Starfleet. The Kai can supposedly explore her guests' 'pagh' (which refers to a person's energy meridian) through deep tissue massage of their ears and this can supposedly reveal a person's true nature. I expect Quark would particularly enjoy this encounter.

In the premiere episode, it is the Kai who reveals to Sisko that he's fated to find the celestial temple, the source of the mysterious and wondrous orbs which are a vital element of the Bajoran religion. According to the DEEP SPACE NINE series bible, "The Kai seems to have an awareness on a higher plane of consciousness, and knows things she cannot possibly know. Although our people do not accept her 'powers' at face value, we cannot always explain them either. She speaks in vague, mystical and indirect language, forcing the listener to seek her meaning."

PITCHING THE SPIN-OFF

These two veterans of STAR TREK: THE NEXT GENERATION had been thinking about creating a new series together for some time. It was Rick Berman, in fact, who first presented Gene Roddenberry with the notion of a NEXT GENERATION spin-off. But Roddenberry died in October of 1991, before he and Berman could discuss the idea at any length. In a famous meeting with Tartikoff and studio executive John Pike, Rick Berman revealed that, by a happy coincidence, he and Michael Piller already had a series concept in the works. Actually, they had more than one: another, non-STAR TREK concept involved a series with a mediaeval setting for its science fiction plots. This was a handy alternative in case Piller and Berman were unable to sway the Paramount studio from its reluctance to do a spin-off of THE NEXT GENERATION.

It was back in October of 1991, when Piller and Berman began developing the show, that they decided to set the series in the same time frame as THE NEXT GENERATION. "That was a decision made consciously to take advantage of all of the alien races; the universe that has been developed over the last five years of THE NEXT GENERATION. We have characters we want to bring onto DEEP SPACE NINE that we've seen on THE NEXT GENERATION. We've got political situations. We've got relationships with the Romulans and the Klingons, and most of all, of course, the Cardassians."

When approval for the spin-off was handed down, the team of Berman and Piller had already done plenty of work on the concept, but now the time had come to really knuckle down. It wasn't as if they had a lot of spare time, either; both men were still actively involved in their respective jobs on STAR TREK: THE NEXT GENERATION, then in its fifth season. In addition to developing DEEP SPACE NINE and writing the pilot, they had to keep working on STAR TREK: THE NEXT GENERATION as well.

VETERAN PRODUCERS

Rick Berman is the absolute boss on STAR TREK: THE NEXT GENERATION in the wake of Gene Roddenberry's passing. On DEEP SPACE NINE, he shares the helm with Michael Piller.

Rick Berman and Michael Piller are both veterans of THE NEXT GENERATION and Piller came on board following experiences writing on staff for the television series SIMON AND SIMON and MIAMI VICE. Piller got involved in television as a journalist. He began in CBS Hollywood checking the accuracy of docudramas. His ambition was to become a producer to protect what he wrote because of all the rewriting which is done to television scripts. Piller had also previously worked on the short-lived science fiction series HARD TIME ON PLANET EARTH.

Michael Piller's job as executive producer of DEEP SPACE NINE primarily involves overseeing the writing and development of ideas for the series. In this capacity he oversees the staff writers and works with the writer of each and every script. Rick Berman participates in that somewhat while he also contributes to Berman's specialty, which is overseeing the production, editing, post-production, music and other aspects of producing the series.

DEEP SPACE NINE producer Michael Piller began his association with the STAR TREK universe when he took charge of the scripting staff for STAR TREK: THE NEXT GENERATION during the third season. He became acquainted with producer Maurice Hurley who invited him to meet with Gene Roddenberry. This led to an episode assignment on THE NEXT GENERATION. Shortly after, Hurley left THE NEXT GENERATION and Piller was invited to join the production staff. "For the next year or so," said Piller, "Gene was really on my case and certainly Rick was on my case. Day after day, we went through the creative process as I began to learn to see life through Gene Roddenberry's eyes. And even as he became sick and trusted Rick and I more and more to execute this vision, to this day, even in death, he is

an extraordinary influence on both of us." He is generally credited with being responsible for the subsequent changes in NEXT GENERATION story development as well as general script improvement. When the shift over to DEEP SPACE NINE came, one of Piller's first tasks was to hire Ira Behr as one of his main writers; he hired Peter Allan Fields away from THE NEXT GENERATION to write as well.

With the advent of the new series, Piller has bowed out of some of his NEXT GENERATION tasks but still maintains control over script development along with executive producer Jeri Taylor. His main focus was on his new project: his goal for DEEP SPACE NINE was to oversee the production of eighteen scripts for the first, short season.

WRITING "EMISSARY"

Piller admits that he was influenced slightly by the NEXT GENERATION pilot, "Encounter at Farpoint," for the DEEP SPACE NINE pilot, "Emissary." Piller took his cue from "Encounter At Farpoint" in delaying the introduction of some key characters until later in the story. (Geordi and Riker only came in much later in the NEXT GENERATION pilot, for instance.)

"Emissary," scripted by Piller from a story by Berman and Piller, would cost as high as twelve million dollars to film (two million of which went to building the standing sets for the series). Obviously, Paramount was more than willing to bank on this project.

Another key plot ingredient inspired by "Encounter At Farpoint" was the necessity of having the lead character (in this case, Benjamin Sisko) explain or justify humanity to an alien race. This may already have become a bit of a cliché in the STAR TREK universe. How many times did Jim Kirk face the same basic problem during his career? It must have run a close second to outsmarting malevolent computers. This time around Piller managed to be give the idea an interesting spin. Sisko must communicate with aliens who do not understand humans and their ilk because they do not, themselves, experience time in a linear fashion (if at all). Sisko is thus faced with the difficult task of explaining time, human consciousness, and the importance of humanity's past experiences to an utterly uncomprehending alien form of consciousness. (One might suspect that these aliens were in fact Kurt Vonnegut's Tralfamadorians out on a lark, but no evidence to support this idea can be found in the pilot as filmed, alas.)

Unfortunately, Piller was dissatisfied with his early versions of the script for "Emissary," and continually involved a somewhat reluctant Rick Berman in constant rehashing of their original story ideas. The basic plot with Sisko explaining humanity to the unseen aliens was, Piller thought, too talky (which brought THE NEXT GENERATION episode "Unification II" to Piller's mind!), and the other aspect of the story— the transition to Federation command of the space station— seemed to be suffering.

In the early concepts of the series, the setting of DEEP SPACE NINE was to have been a dilapidated, seedy space station with technology that lagged somewhat behind that of the Federation. In the course of series development, this notion had been scrapped in favor of a more high-tech look. Now, however, Piller was forced to re-think his whole approach.

The Los Angeles riots of 1992 gave Piller his breakthrough idea. While the station would still be a fairly advanced piece of alien technology, Piller decided that the departing Cardassians would ransack the place, leaving a shambles that Sisko would be faced with rebuilding. Now the new commander's job would involve convincing the merchants of the Promenade, and other inhabitants of the station, to stay and pull things back together.

This, in turn, helped Piller to develop the relationship between Security Chief Odo (Rene Auberjonois) and the Ferengi huckster Quark (Armin Shimerman).

RICK BERMAN

Rick Berman is quick to insist that the creation of DEEP SPACE NINE has in no way diminished the quality of STAR TREK: THE NEXT GENERATION. Claiming the sixth season of THE NEXT GENERATION as one of the best yet.

Ignoring the theory, expounded by certain cynics, that THE NEXT GENERATION is being made worse intentionally in order to draw bored fans' attention to DEEP SPACE NINE, Berman is hopeful that both series will claim a sizable audience, pointing out that there are considerable differences between the two series. DEEP SPACE NINE is not, after all, a carbon copy of THE NEXT GENERATION.

HERMAN ZIMMERMAN

Herman Zimmerman comes to DEEP SPACE NINE with a strong STAR TREK background: after all, he designed the first season for STAR TREK: THE NEXT GENERATION, as well as working on the feature films STAR TREK V: THE FINAL FRONTIER and STAR TREK VI: THE UNDISCOVERED COUNTRY. After five years away from television, he responded eagerly when Berman asked him to work on the set design for the new series.

Sets for "Emissary" cost more than those for STAR TREK VI: THE UNDISCOVERED COUNTRY: a whopping two million dollars! And under Zimmerman's guidance, the DEEP SPACE NINE sets were created from scratch. This was, after all, to be a new setting for a series. With no reference point for Cardassian architecture, it was necessary for Zimmerman and his team to invent it out of thin air.

CARDASSIAN POST-MODERN

In designing the Cardassian architecture, Zimmerman was inspired by the Cardassian look already established on THE NEXT GENERATION. Unfortunately, even this was limited, as the interior of the Cardassian ships had never been seen. So Zimmerman drew primarily from Bob Blackman's design for Cardassian costuming, an armored look was that somewhat crustacean in appearance. Part of the theory was that the Cardassians were big on structure, and if Cardassians felt structure was of vital importance, they would (like a crab, Zimmerman reasoned) keep structures on the outside. Zimmerman visualized a space station whose basic framework was not concealed inside, as in human architecture, but one where all supports and structures were clearly visible both inside the sets and with outside views of the entire station.

Working with Zimmerman's basic concept, Nathan Cowley and Joe Hodges melded the desired crustacean concept with the heavy-handed impressiveness of Fascist architecture for the show's sets. As finally realized, the sets are quite imposing, but they still have their own unique appeal, a strangely alien sort of streamlining. Cardassian Post-modernism if you will.

As the Cardassians are very military, their Command/Ops center (which combines all the features of Transporter room, engineering and command functions in one central location) was placed by Zimmerman in such a fashion that the commander's office can look down on it and see everything that is going on. There are literally windows everywhere in that office, so that the Cardassian commander would have had no blind spots whatsoever. The Cardassians commander's staff must have been very uncomfortable indeed under his watchful gaze.

A HOSTILE ENVIRONMENT

Part of Zimmerman's design concept was that the sets and devices on the Cardassian-built station were not as "user-friendly" as those on, say, the Enterprise. Perhaps most notable are the automatic doors on DS9. These are large, round, cog-wheeled doors that roll noisily out of the way and then roll ominously shut. One gets the feeling that, while the smooth, almost soundless doors on board the Enterprise would not, and almost certainly could not, close on you, it seems likely that Cardassian safety features were not so rigorous, and that being caught in the way of one of these portals would really hurt.

In fact, this ties in with another underlying design concept. This is, after all, an alien space station, and it is doubtful whether any of the Federation personnel on board will ever be able to get used to living on DS9. Another factor contributing to this feeling is the imposing size of the sets for the show; looming bulkheads and support beams at odd angles everywhere, windows not quite shaped or set at the right level for humans and those damned doors just waiting to catch the heel of a slow-moving Ferengi.

To further enhance this off-balance sensation, Zimmerman designed a large viewscreen (larger than the one he created for the Enterprise of THE NEXT GENERATION) that could be seen from both sides for DS9's operations center. This device is turned on only when needed. Gone is the Enterprise's familiar view of the stars, which always cuts back in when communications are terminated. On DS9, you actually see the viewscreen go off. A ring of blue neon (which necessitates shooting the effect with a green screen) gives a blurred edge to the viewscreen image, enhancing the alien look to its technology.

DETAILS, DETAILS, DETAILS

Another aspect of on-set effects that sets DEEP SPACE NINE apart from THE NEXT GENERATION is its use of real-time video monitors on the set with actual video images. This was made feasible by the development of techniques which can reduce video speed (a standard thirty frames-per-second) to the motion picture standard (twenty-four frames per second). With the image speeds matched in this fashion, it is now possible to film live video monitors without any image distortion. This is so effective that there are nearly seventy on-line video screens in use on the sets of DEEP SPACE NINE. The total cost?: nearly forty-five thousand dollars!

Another interesting detail can be found in the Holo-suites above the Promenade. Paramount's PR people insist (a bit too loudly, perhaps) that they are not being used for any sort of sexual activities. Unfortunately the actors state otherwise, particularly Armin Shimmerman. Plus the episode "Move Along Home" makes it very clear in the dialogue that this is exactly what the holo-suites are used for. Again, in keeping with the Cardassian design concept, they reveal the bulky holograph-producing machinery when they are shut off, as opposed to the clean yellow grid pattern seen when an Enterprise holodeck shuts down on THE NEXT GENERATION.

DESIGNING EFFECTS: RICHARD DELGADO

The opening title sequence of DEEP SPACE NINE was visually realized by special effects maven Dan Curry (whose NEXT GENERATION credits are lengthy). The sequence itself was designed and storyboarded by Richard Delgado, an illustrator whose bosses are Herman Zimmerman and Rick Sternbach. Pre-production illustrations are Delgado's specialty. Much of the look of DEEP SPACE NINE can be directly attributed to this talented artist, who came to the new series with no previous experience working on a Trek-related project.

Influenced largely by the work of French artist Jean Giraud (a.k.a. Moebius), Delgado designed many of the

essential but unobtrusive background details of many of the show's sets in his meticulous designs. An interplanetary banking station and a Twenty-Fourth Century ATM was incorporated into the Promenade set and built directly from Delgado's designs. In fact, much of the Promenade was the creation of Delgado, from alien plants to shop designs. The only complaint Delgado seems to have about his job is that his boss, Herman Zimmerman, seems to find Delgado's sketches more effective when turned upside down.

Bunks in the former Cardassian quarters were also Delgado's design. Although not yet used on screen, Cardassian bunk beds come equipped with a force field, in case someone tries to assassinate the sleeper. This too was Delgado's idea.

The actual design of the space station exterior (the largest version being a six-foot model) was the work of many hands. Other hands beside those of Delgado contributed to its design, including those of Rick Sternbach, Mike Okuda, set designers Joe Hodges and Nathan Crowley, and scenic artists Denise Okuda and Doug Drexler.

FILMING DS9 : MARVIN RUSH

DEEP SPACE NINE's chief of photography is none other than Marvin Rush, who held that same position on THE NEXT GENERATION for three seasons. (Rush's job on THE NEXT GENERATION has been assumed by the talented cameraman Jonathan West.) In switching shows, Rush finds himself faced with a job of an entirely different scale.

What faces him is this fact: the sets for DEEP SPACE NINE are radically different from those for STAR TREK: THE NEXT GENERATION. They are much larger. New sets on recent NEXT GENERATION episodes have been things along the lines of Jeffrey Tubes intersections and the like. There are no new, large structures likely to turn up on the Enterprise (despite the many visually unexplored areas on board that immense ship). This is clearly not the state of things on DEEP SPACE NINE. Utilizing sets on three sound stages at Paramount Studios, including Sound Stages Four and Seventeen, DEEP SPACE NINE boasts two large, multiple-leveled sets: the Ops Center and Quark's Promenade. These sets are built more in the manner of feature film sets. Paramount has been more than willing to lavish large sums of money on the series they hope will be another smash syndication success for them.

These sets present a wide range of filming options. Camera moves on the large, sometimes complicated sets of DS9 are not so simple. This presents a much wider range of options in terms of camera movement and techniques than is generally permitted by THE NEXT GENERATION's format rules.

On one hand, DEEP SPACE NINE has much more room for crane shots than THE NEXT GENERATION ever allowed. (Luckily, Rick Berman is no Guy Caballero in this department.) On the other hand, the cameras on DEEP SPACE NINE may on many occasions be obliged to make a sudden transition from the wide-open spaces of the Promenade to the dim, cramped spaces of one of the many small shops which fill that space. While very large, the space station DS9 has many obscure corners. All in all, there are many challenges waiting for Marvin Rush and his DEEP SPACE NINE camera crew.

MICHAEL WESTMORE: ALIEN CREATOR

Like producers Rick Berman and Michael Piller, Emmy winning makeup artist Michael Westmore now has two full time jobs: THE NEXT GENERATION and DEEP SPACE NINE. Fortunately, he has an able staff of assistants to help him out on DS9: Craig Reardon, Jill Rockow and Janna Phillips. Janna Phillips is the daughter of Fred Phillips, the very first STAR TREK makeup artist. The man who designed the ears of Spock himself!

DEEP SPACE NINE calls for so many aliens that Westmore is no longer constrained by THE NEXT GENERATION's rule that new aliens must be designed for a specific script. On DEEP SPACE NINE, he can create aliens at will. Some will wind up as characters, and some will become an essential part of the background scenery.

One such character is the hulking Lurian, an alien who has been seen but not really included in any plotlines yet. This far he/it seems to be one of Quark's most reliable bar customers— sort of the Norm Petersen of the Twenty-Fourth Century. Some creatures created for DEEP SPACE NINE have also shown up in Ten Forward on THE NEXT GENERATION, raising the interesting question—are some of these creatures simply intergalactic bar hoppers out on a never ending binge?

Some aliens from THE NEXT GENERATION also show up on DEEP SPACE NINE. Viewers of the pilot episode, "Emissary," undoubtedly noticed that one of Benjamin Sisko's command officers during the battle with the Borg was a blue skinned Bolin, a race first encountered on THE NEXT GENERATION in the character of Captain Picard's talkative barber.

The most prominent NEXT GENERATION alien crossover (after the Ferengi and the Cardassians) is the character of Jadzia Dax, who is a member of the Trill— a race first encountered in the NEXT GENERATION episode "The Host."

The Trill ambassador featured in that episode had a significantly different appearance than Dax does: it was more of a nose and forehead make-up effect which was dropped for the Trill character on DEEP SPACE NINE. For her portrayal of Jadzia Dax, Terry Farrell, fortunately, does not need to hide her attractive features behind any sort of appliance. In her case her "Trillness" derives from her spots, which start at her hairline and run down the side of her face, her neck and presumably beyond. In "Emissary," a glimpse is had of more of her spots, at least as far down as the top of her shoulders. Westmore applies the spotting himself on a daily basis.

As if to compensate for the change in Trill appearance, Westmore's facial appliance for Rene Auberjonois' shape-shifting character of Odo is quite an extensive prosthetic, one that effectively "runs" his facial features together.

And so, with a brilliant team at work, all the elements needed to get DEEP SPACE NINE on the air are in place: script, sets, special effects, actors and their make-up. A major investment for Paramount, and a labor of love for all involved, the new series looks great, and promises to be a worthy addition to the ongoing legacy of Gene Roddenberry's lasting creation.

Fully a year and a half before DEEP SPACE NINE went on the air, the groundwork was being laid to expand the STAR TREK universe in ways that a third series could take advantage of.

LAYING THE GROUNDWORK— FROM NEXT GENERATION TO DEEP SPACE NINE

While DEEP SPACE NINE is the latest addition to the STAR TREK canon, its precedents can be found in the series that preceded it, THE NEXT GENERATION. Many key elements of DEEP SPACE NINE are encountered originally in episodes of THE NEXT GENERATION: The Ferengi, the Cardassians, and the Bajorans all first appeared in that series. A brief look back at their previous histories will undoubtedly shed some interesting light on the goings-on that take place under Benjamin Sisko's command on the space station designated Deep Space Nine.

DEVOLUTION OF THE FERENGI

Gene Roddenberry had great hopes for the Ferengi: he envisioned them as the villains of THE NEXT GENERATION, and put a great deal of thought into their character. Motivated utterly by greed, they were to be utterly ruthless in their pursuit of material gain, deadly foes despite their somewhat comical appearance.

Viewers of THE NEXT GENERATION got their first glimpse of the Ferengi in "The Last Outpost," which was the fifth episode of the series. Armin Shimerman played Letek, one of the Ferengi, marking his first— but not last— time out as a member of this race. Shimerman would eventually be cast as Quark on DEEP SPACE NINE, a reward for his long association with the Ferengi.

In "The Last Outpost," the Ferengi have never been seen, although there have been a few encounters with their ships— as would be seen in a later episode. Here they come across as fairly ruthless, attacking Riker and an Away Team with deadly whips. The episode also involves a slumbering alien consciousness which eventually awakens. In typical STAR TREK fashion, it judges the character of the persons disturbing it, finding Riker to be civilized. The entity even offers to destroy the Ferengi, but Riker passes on this. The Ferengi remind him of how humans were two centuries earlier.

The Ferengi reappeared in "The Battle," another first season episode. Here they were still pretty much villains. We also learn that it was a battle with a Ferengi ship that led to Picard's loss of his previous command, the Stargazer. A Ferengi ship returns the wreck of the Stargazer to Picard, ostensibly as a peace offering, but actually as part of a revenge plot. Daimon Bock, commander of the Ferengi ship, is the father of the captain of the ship that attacked the Stargazer years before. His son died at the Battle of Maxia, as it came to be called. His plot to discredit Picard, and to drive him insane, almost works, but it is thwarted. Bock is relieved of command by a subordinate because his private vendetta violated Ferengi ethics in one crucial way: it was not profitable.

THE FERENGI: FEARSOME OR ANNOYING?

By this time Roddenberry and his associates had come to the conclusion that the Ferengi were not the heavies that he'd hoped they would be, and they disappeared for quite some time, making only one appearance during the second season.

Notable in the fact that Armin Shimerman again appeared as a Ferengi, "Peak Performance" was perhaps the best episode so far to feature the Ferengi, although here they were not so much villains as greedy buffoons who stumbled into a wargame exercise between the Enterprise and another ship commanded by Riker. Thinking that the wargame is a real conflict between two Federation ships, the Ferengi suspect that something valuable is involved, and cut in, complicating matters. This established the tone of future Ferengi encounters: although their interference provided danger, they themselves were more irritating than threatening.

The third season saw no less than three Ferengi outings, all of which cast the Ferengi as greedy buffoons who figure in plot development but are in no way true antagonists— just nuisances. In "The Price," they interfered in important trade negotiations by inducing an allergic reaction in a Federation negotiator. In "Captain's Holiday," Max Grodenchik (who would eventually be cast as Quark's brother on DEEP SPACE NINE) portrayed a Ferengi who, along with a few other characters, undermines Jean-Luc Picard's plans for a quiet vacation. "Ménage a Troi" revealed another aspect of the Ferengi personality: they're extremely horny (and their ears are erogenous zones). In this particular outing, perhaps the most farcical episode of THE NEXT GENERATION, a Ferengi captain falls head over heels in lust with Lwaxana Troi, and kidnaps her, Deanna and Riker.

After a complete dearth of Ferengi episodes during the fourth season of THE NEXT GENERATION, they returned briefly in the fifth season episode "The Perfect Mate." Here, two extremely stupid Ferengi, motivated by greed, set the plot in motion but have nothing more to do with the story.

ONE LAST STAB AT VILLAINDOM

Then, the Ferengi actually returned as villains of a sort in the sixth season outing "Rascals." In this tale, some very serious Ferengi outlaws actually succeed in hijacking the Enterprise. By a fortuitous plot coincidence, however, Picard and three other regular characters have been turned into children, while retaining their adult minds, and use the Ferengi disregard for children to their disadvantage and save the ship.

As can be seen from this brief survey, the Ferengi have suffered a great deal at the hands of the creators of THE NEXT GENERATION, who seem unable to make up their mind about what to do with them. But they saw fit to cast a Ferengi as a regular on DEEP SPACE NINE. This may actually be a good move; with a single actor playing the same Ferengi every week, there is at last an opportunity to develop the character of that race, and its interactions with the Federation.

ENTER THE CARDASSIANS

For the villains of DEEP SPACE NINE, Berman and Piller chose the Cardassians. The are a warlike race who were introduced in the fourth season episode "The Wounded." Directed by Chip Chalmers from a script by Jeri Taylor, "The Wounded" examined the aftermath of a recently resolved conflict between the Federation and the Cardassians. It is revealed that Chief O'Brien had once been involved in face-to-face combat with Cardassians and had in fact killed one in self defense, which goes against his general nature.

"The Wounded" began when the Enterprise was fired upon by a Cardassian vessel. This is perplexing since the Cardassians have signed a treaty with the Federation, not only ending the conflict between these two sociopolitical spheres of influence but ostensibly creating an alliance between them.

Picard discovers that the peace had been broken by a Federation officer, Ben Maxwell, who is in command of the Federation ship Phoenix. Apparently, Maxwell, unable to cope with the death of his family in a border skirmish with the Cardassians, is unwilling to accept the new peace treaty. He has dropped out of contact with the Federation and embarked on a personal vendetta against their former enemies. His first assault resulted in the destruction of a Cardassian science station.

Picard is ordered to investigate the situation and to bring Maxwell back under rein. The Cardassians have agreed to temporarily suspend their disbelief and accept the personal vengeance scenario, but, being untrusting, they invoke a clause in the treaty and send an observation team along with Picard.

SHADOWS FROM THE PAST

Chief O'Brien is somewhat disturbed by the presence of Cardassians aboard. To complicate matters for him, O'Brien is the only Enterprise crew member to have served under Maxwell during the period of hostilities, and is brought into the situation. His own battle experience is revealed; O'Brien has trouble dealing with the Cardassians, not because he hates them, but because they remind him of his only act of aggression against another living being.

The Enterprise's sensors eventually locate the Phoenix, but they arrive too late to stop Maxwell from destroying a Cardassian warship and freighter. Pursuing at high warp speed, the Enterprise catches up with the Phoenix. Maxwell reveals to Picard that he is acting under the belief that the Cardassians are using the new peace as a pretext to re-arm for an even greater course of aggression against the Federation. Maxwell is clearly disturbed but finally agrees to return to Federation space if Picard will allow him to retain command of the Phoenix.

Soon enough, however, the Phoenix breaks away from the Enterprise and heads toward another Cardassian freighter. Rather than destroy this vessel outright, Maxwell gives Picard the option of boarding the ship and seeing that it does, as Maxwell believes, indeed contain armaments. This would put Picard in the position of breaking the treaty. But if Picard does not follow this course of action, Maxwell will destroy the freighter. Playing for time, Picard stalls, threatening to fire on the Phoenix, while O'Brien devises a means of beaming over to the Phoenix during a break in the shield's oscillation cycle. Successful in this attempt, O'Brien manages to talk his former commander out of his untenable position. Maxwell finally surrenders to Picard and beams over to the Enterprise.

The head of the Cardassian observers thanks Picard for his skillful resolution of the situation. But Picard turns the tables by revealing that he and the Federation believe that Maxwell is really correct about the Cardassian rearmament effort. Maxwell was stopped in order to preserve the peace. The Federation, however, will be keeping a close eye on the Cardassians from this point on.

CARDASSIANS VS. BAJORANS

Drawing on the Cardassian background, Rick Berman and Berman Piller began to use the fifth season of THE NEXT GENERATION as a means of lay-

ing the groundwork for DEEP SPACE NINE.

They decided to create a new character for THE NEXT GENERATION who would provide an introduction to the culture of the Bajorans. This character, portrayed by Michelle Forbes, would debut in the episode which bore her name, "Ensign Ro." Scripted by Michael Piller from a story by himself and Rick Berman, this episode introduces the planet Bajor and reveals its long-standing troubles with the Cardassians.

The episode begins with Picard getting a haircut when the Enterprise receives an urgent distress signal from the Solarian Four colony, which is located near the Cardassian border. The message is abruptly terminated and cannot be re-established. Sensors detect a vessel departing from the ruins of Solarian Four. This ship broadcasts a message claiming that the colony had been destroyed by Bajoran freedom fighters.

The Enterprise takes the survivors of the attack to a space station. There, Picard is met by an Admiral Kennelly, who discusses the attack with him. The Admiral has a cold, which he caught from the Cardassian liaison who was at the station. A brief review of local history reveals that the Cardassians, a rather imperialistic people, had annexed the Bajoran homeworld some forty years ago, making interplanetary refugees of countless Bajorans.

Kennelly suspects that the attack was the work of the Bajoran terrorist leader Orta, and assigns Picard to locate Orta and use his diplomatic skills to halt Orta's attacks on Federation outposts. Previously, Orta and his freedom fighters had only attacked Cardassian targets.

ENSIGN RO

Kennelly has Ensign Ro Laren, a Federation officer from Bajor, transferred to the Enterprise. As a Starfleet officer, she was court marshaled several years earlier for an incident on Garon Two, where she disobeyed orders; eight members of her Away Team died, perhaps not as a direct result of her actions, but the weight of their deaths has become a blot on her career. She has been imprisoned up until the time that Admiral Kennelly reinstates her. Picard is angry at this transfer as it was made without consulting him. Commander Riker dislikes the idea as well. He and Picard both distrust Ro, but the Admiral insists that she is crucial to their effort to locate the elusive Orta.

When Ro reports for duty she makes it clear that she doesn't like the assignment either, but that it is better than staying in prison. Still, she wants the assignment out of the way just as quickly as Picard and Riker do.

The Enterprise visits Valo Three to meet with Jas Holza at a Bajoran refugee camp. They hope he can help them reach the terrorist, Orta. But Ro says that Jas is a figurehead and recommends talking to someone else. (Note: Bajorans list their surnames first, like the Japanese traditionally do, a fact which Ensign Ro frequently finds it necessary to point out to the uninformed.) Beaming down, they meet Keeve Falor, who swears that he won't help the Federation because they have used the Prime Directive as an excuse to allow the Cardassians to repress and dispossess the Bajorans. Picard is troubled by the conditions he observes in the Bajoran refugee camps and orders blankets and medical supplies to be sent immediately. Reassessing Picard's character after this action, Keeve agrees to help.

DOUBLE AGENT

Ro is a contentious and abrasive personality who stands out in comparison to the other Enterprise personnel. This draws Guinan's attention to her when she visits Ten Forward. Ro prefers to sit alone, but Guinan presses the question of what really happened on Garon Two, which annoys Ro. Ro finally leaves when a subspace message arrives for her, leaving a bemused Guinan behind.

Taking the message in her quarters, Ro converses with Admiral Kennelly; it becomes obvious that she is on a personal mission for the Admiral, and one that is quite different from the one that Picard believes himself to be carrying out.

In time, the Enterprise arrives at the third moon of Valo One, where Ro secretly beams down six hours ahead of schedule. When this is discovered, a furious Commander Riker fumes as Picard and his Away Team transport down to find her. The Away Team is taken prisoner by Orta's Bajoran terrorists; Orta is willing to talk with Picard but distrusts the Federation. To further cloud the issues at hand, Orta denies any involvement in the attack on Solarian Four, leaving Picard to wonder: could someone else be trying to draw the Federation into the conflict between the Bajorans and the Cardassians?

Picard is furious with Ensign Ro and restricts her to her quarters for violating protocol. Guinan visits Ro and, learning of her predicament, convinces her to reveal the truth to Captain Picard. Guinan brings Ro to the Captain where she confesses that Admiral Kennelly had assigned her to this mission to pursue a second, secret goal: to offer arms to the Bajorans— a clear violation of Federation policy.

THE TRAITOR REVEALED

Ro reveals that she hates the Cardassians because when she was seven years old she was forced to watch them torture her father to death. Picard accepts her revelations and asks her to convince Orta to go along with a plan which could expose the conspiracy. The Enterprise then contacts Admiral Kennelly and tells him that they've made a deal with Orta and are about to escort Orta's ship to a Bajoran camp on Valo Three.

During the voyage, the Enterprise detects two Cardassian warships. The Enterprise intercepts the Cardassians, who demand that the ship full of Bajoran terrorists be turned over to them, giving the Enterprise one hour to withdraw. Picard contacts the Admiral, telling him that the Cardassians seemed to have rather precise knowledge of the course taken by Orta and his escort. Kennelly tells Picard to give up the Bajorans, rather than offend the Cardassians and undermine the alliance. Picard accuses the Cardassians of plotting to involve the Federation in their war, but he obeys Kennelly and withdraws, allowing the Cardassians to destroy Orta's vessel.

Kennelly contacts Picard again, only to discover that the Bajoran transport ship had been a decoy; Orta and his people were not actually on the empty vessel. Picard reveals that he has evidence now to prove that the Solarian Four incident was staged by the Cardassians, largely in an effort to enlist Kennelly's assistance in their plan to destroy Orta. For his part in all this, Admiral Kennelly will face a court martial.

Impressed by Ensign Ro, Picard invites her to remain in Starfleet and to serve under his command. She is reluctant, but agrees to do so as long as Picard allows her to wear her traditional Bajoran earring, which the captain had earlier prohibited as a violation of Starfleet uniform regulations.

WHITHER ENSIGN RO?

The character of Ensign Ro was well received, and Michelle Forbes would reprise it throughout the fifth season as well as (briefly) the sixth. However, any plans to have her step over to DEEP SPACE NINE were scuttled when the talented actress proved unwilling to commit to full time series work. While perfectly willing to appear as a frequent guest star, Forbes wanted to keep her options open for any possible film work that might come her way (such as the forthcoming feature movie KALIFORNIA). Apparently, she has now been dropped from THE NEXT GENERATION; her last appearance as Ensign Ro was in the episode "Rascals," where she was one of the characters turned into children.

Actually, the role of Ro, although created as part of the groundwork for DEEP SPACE NINE, had not specifically been intended to cross over to the new show. Efforts to talk Forbes into committing to a single season (there was talk of killing her off at the end of the first year!) yielded nothing, leading Michael Piller, already re-writing the pilot for DEEP SPACE NINE, to create a new character to take her place.

Still, Michelle Forbes remains a part of the STAR TREK universe. In her second appearance on THE NEXT GENERATION, she was one of the Enterprise crew members stranded on the bridge in "Disaster." Things really got complicated for her in "Conundrum," when the entire Enterprise crew suffer a mysterious amnesia; all Ro Laren recalls is her attraction to Commander Riker, which leads to a steamy romance amidst all the other confusion— and considerable embarrassment for Riker when normalcy is restored. In "Power Play" she was Geordi's primary ally in the struggle to free Deanna Troi, Chief O'Brien and Data from the alien entities that have possessed them. After a largely supporting role in "Cause and Effect," she again teamed with Geordi LaForge in "The Next Phase," in which a Romulan plot causes both characters to vanish to the eyes of everyone but each other. While struggling with a Romulan in the same situation, they try to somehow get Data's attention, and actually attend their own funerals before they are restored to their proper place.

Ro Laren's part in the sixth season of THE NEXT GENERATION, limited mostly to being turned into a child along with Picard, Guinan and Keiko O'Brien, was brief. And only her initial appearance in "Ensign Ro" had anything to do with the fact that she was Bajoran. One can only imagine what DEEP SPACE NINE would have been like with her participation. Perhaps she will return as a guest on one program or another. Until then it is to be hoped that she will find success in her career, wherever it may lead her.

INTO DEEP SPACE

And now, DEEP SPACE NINE goes forward. With the strong backgrounds of the Cardassian and Bajoran races to draw from, there should be many opportunities for exciting drama on the new series. And the Ferengi, as usual, are a wild card. It would be impossible to guess what Quark will be up to in the future, as he is a completely amoral character, acting always to his financial advantage. Certainly, DEEP SPACE NINE could have been created out of whole cloth. By utilizing pieces of NEXT GENERATION back-history, the new series has not only a surefire audience, but a consistent link with the on-going saga of the STAR TREK universe.

What is the corner of the galaxy like where the space station Deep Space Nine resides? What are the Bajorans like as a culture and how does their recent history impact on what is happening now?

SPECIAL CORNER OF THE GALAXY: THE REALM OF DEEPSPACE NINE

When DEEP SPACE NINE opens, it is at a turning point. Bajor has just regained its independence following a long, despotic rule and has requested admission into the Federation. Bajor was annexed by the Cardassians four decades before. But the Cardassians were anything but benevolent despots. [Note: Some sources, including the DEEP SPACE NINE writers/directors guide, incorrectly states that the Cardassians ruled Bajor for 100 years. But in the fifth season TNG episode "Ensign Ro" it was established that it was forty years. This takes priority over all subsequent mentions.]

The longer the Cardassians controlled the planet, the more difficult the Bajorans became to control. They increasingly resisted the exploitation of their world with nothing being returned to benefit its people. This inevitably led to violent resistance in the form of an underground of Bajoran terrorists. The presence of the terrorists, combined with the Cardassians completing their stripping Bajor of all its useful resources, made the conquerors decide to withdraw and leave the Bajorans to fend for themselves. After forty years of plundering, the planet had nothing left worth stealing, or so they believed.

However, the Cardassians didn't leave quietly. As though their brutal rule was not enough, before they left they destroyed everything they could. Water supplies were poisoned, cities ravaged and burned out, and even the ancient monastery, the heart of the Bajoran planet's religion, was desecrated. If the Bajorans were finally going to achieve freedom, it would be at the greatest cost the Cardassians could extract.

BAJOR—STARTING OVER

Once the Cardassians finally withdrew, the Bajorans reluctantly turned to the Federation and requested admittance. But this was hardly a popular decision. Decades of alien rule has made many Bajorans mistrustful of foreign entanglements. Some of the terrorist underground fear that the Federation, with all its might, could all too easily step in and pick up where the Cardassians left off. Age old political factions, once united in opposition to the Cardassians, have splintered once again and resumed old conflicts. They've taken sides both for and against admittance to the Federation.

It is only because of the obviously weakened state of Bajor, and its desperate need of assistance, that has held the most radical elements of these political factions in check. Even so, some individuals are not above attempting to display their contempt for the Federation and any sort of alien alliances. Better to be free standing than to be ruled by even a benevolent dictator. Starfleet has remained true to their promise to have only an advisory presence, although their scientific expertise has placed them in a command position aboard Deep Space Nine.

Starfleet's mission to Bajor is to spearhead the arduous diplomatic and scientific efforts that accompany the lengthy entry procedure into the Federation. All of this was complicated infinitely when the stable wormhole was discovered near Bajor.

THE SECRET OF THE WORMHOLE

A wormhole is essentially a shortcut through space. Upon entering one end of the wormhole one almost immediately exists from the other end billions of kilometers away. A trip that would take months, years or perhaps be otherwise impossible can be made in seconds. Previous wormholes which were encountered proved to be unstable. They would disappear almost as abruptly as they appeared, with entrance and exit points changing. But the first stable wormhole, which is discovered near the Denorios asteroid field, turns out to be close to Bajor and is not discovered until after the Cardassians have left. Like any wormhole, it is only visible when an object enters or exits through it.

The Bajoran wormhole will take a starship, or even something as simple as a runabout shuttle, to the Gamma Quadrant, which would otherwise have been a sixty year journey at warp nine, presuming that one could build a starship capable of maintaining warp nine for six decades. Upon entering the wormhole, brilliant colors appear which surround the ship. Inside, strange visual distortions affect the perceptions of the passengers as they plunge through the space-time continuum.

This newly discovered wormhole opens up a passageway to the hundreds of unexplored worlds in the Gamma Quadrant. Not only is the Federation sending ships through to make contact with them, but ships from the Gamma

Quadrant are coming through to make contact with Deep Space Nine. This has turned the backwater and commerce starved planet of Bajor into a crossroads of both trade and scientific exploration. This is attracting travelers from all over the galaxy who otherwise would have had no reason to come there. For a planet depleted of its natural resources, this is a godsend which will insure that Bajor will be able to rebuild after the long years of destructive Cardassian rule.

The reason that this wormhole was unknown until after the Cardassians left is that it was artificially created by a species of aliens who live on a world inside the wormhole. They do not occupy the same time-space continuum as the rest of the known inhabited planets do. In fact they have no concept of past or future as for them all of time exists simultaneously until Ben Sisko makes them understand how his species lives in a linear timeline. These aliens have been sending out mysterious orbs (one every century for a thousand years) in their attempts to contact other life forms. Sisko was the first who used one to contact them. These orbs have become important religious artifacts to the Bajorans and are among the fundamental sacrament of the Bajoran religion.

CREATION OF DEEP SPACE NINE

The Federation managed to prevent the Cardassians from returning to Bajor once the wormhole is discovered. But due to the continued turmoil on Bajor among its political factions, the Federation doesn't consider it safe to establish a physical presence on the surface of the planet itself. But at the request of the provisional government, Starfleet takes command of the abandoned Cardassian space station which is in orbit around Bajor. The station is moved into a larger orbit which places it close to the entrance to the wormhole. This way it can be guarded against undue exploitation or control by any hostile species. But the station, called Deep Space Nine, remains the property of Bajor even though it is administered by Starfleet in the form of Commander Ben Sisko.

Deep Space Nine had been haphazardly assembled by the Cardassians over several years using Bajoran work teams. It was used primarily by the Cardassians to monitor mining operations on Bajor and to service the incoming and outgoing crews. About two hundred people, mostly Bajorans, still reside there, plus about fifty Starfleet officers and crewmen.

When the Cardassians abandoned Bajor, they stripped the station of all advanced technology and defense capabilities. This left Starfleet with the demanding task of making the station fully operational once more. But because the Cardassians knew what to take, not everything on the station can be made fully functional without running into recurring glitches.

The Operations Control Center (OPS), the heart of Deep Space Nine, is a multi-leveled facility lined with computer and life support systems, tactical controls, the master communications panel and a Transporter pad to beam on and off the station. It is always a hub of activity as ships move in and out of the wormhole. There are shuttle bays for smaller vessels while the larger ships must dock close by while the starship crews have access to the space station via airlocks and interconnecting tunnels.

A HUB OF ACTIVITY

Due to the presence of the wormhole, anywhere from ten to three hundred visitors arrive at the station as vessels arrive containing merchants, scientists, explorers as well as spies and others who have criminal intent. While most visitors remain quartered aboard their ships, the station also has some special guest quarters. All visiting ships have to stop off at Deep Space Nine in order to be retrofitted with special impulse energy buffers which allow the vessels to travel safely through the wormhole. This is because the ordinary power sources the vessels use are destructive to the ionic field where the aliens who created the wormhole live.

The spacecraft available for general use by the personnel of the station are called Runabouts, and Starfleet has stationed three mid-sized Runabout Class patrol ships at Deep Space Nine. These ships have the capability of carrying personnel to star systems within this sector as well as through the wormhole itself. The Runabout Class ships are twenty meters long and have both impulse and warp capabilities. The Runabout can achieve a maximum warp speed of 4.7. They are small, like shuttles, and are sometimes referred to as shuttles by the personnel. They are generally operated by a two man crew but a single person can pilot one when necessary. A Runabout is capable of transporting up to forty people in a tight squeeze. The sleeping quarters about a Runabout will fit six people but are both cramped and uncomfortable.

The Runabouts are not built for luxury by any stretch. Directly off the cockpit is a multi-purpose room which can be used for either meetings or dining. The Runabouts are the only overt symbol of Federation presence in the sector. Due to the politically charged atmosphere on Bajor, no starship is on permanent duty. The powerful armaments would make the recently independent Bajorans nervous as such a vessel would seem to be a silent symbol of the restrictions which Starfleet could easily impose if they chose to do so.

LIFE IN THE PROMENADE

In some ways life aboard Deep Space Nine is very similar to the way it was when the Cardassians were in charge. The Cardassians had sold the rights for commercial concessions on the station to the highest bidder. Those who won the concession rights were able to provide exclusive services to the mining crews who passed through the station on their way both on and off the planet. Since the Cardassians were stripping the planet of all its wealth, that took a lot of miners to operate a lot of machinery. The focal point of this commerce on Deep Space Nine is the Promenade.

The Promenade is supposed to be something between a free port and a flea market which is bustling with aliens of all sorts. There's gambling, smuggling and the worst sort of chicanery going on. The Cardassians didn't care what happened there so long as they were paid their cut. But as a nod towards keeping the peace with their unwilling servants, the Cardassians allowed a Bajoran temple there as well. Other delights included a kiosk which serves live food, a specialty that the Ferengi particularly enjoy.

The hub of activity on the Promenade is Quark's place, a bar and gambling emporium which has a brothel upstairs in the form of holodeck suites whose programming can satisfy the desire of any known intelligent species. A Ferengi, Quark, owns and operates the club. He fits right in with the atmosphere the Cardassians created because Quark was just as ruthless and untrustworthy as the average Cardassian. They respected Quark and therefore didn't trash his establishment the way they did everything else on the station when they left. The Cardassians liked Quark, which is one of the reasons Sisko and Odo continue to mistrust him.

When the Cardassians declared Bajor a loss and pulled out, Quark was considering leaving as well, believing that the Federation would put too many restrictions on him to make his business profitable. But Commander Sisko assured Quark that he would not be bothered so long as he didn't get too out of hand or engage in flagrantly illegal activity. In other words, so long as he didn't get caught. But the Federation doesn't have guards posted to insure that no one is cheated. Sisko made the deal with Quark in order to keep all of the merchants on the Promenade from leaving, and thereby devastating the economy of the station and making it unattractive for visitors. By staying, Quark showed that what was left was worth saving as everyone knew that where a Ferengi does business has to be profitable or he wouldn't bother staying around. This was, of course, before the wormhole was discovered. After that, no one needed to be convinced to keep their businesses open on Deep Space Nine.

BAJOR

The world which the station is closest to, and which it had until recently been in a tight orbit around, is Bajor. Bajor is an ancient society dedicated to spiritual pursuits. The mysterious orbs seen in "The Emissary" indicate some of what that religion involves. An old planet with an ancient culture, its people are just coming out from under the brutal Cardassian domination and are rebuilding what had been damaged or lost under that ruthless dictatorship. Bajor is a world of striking architecture with rounded domes and other spherical shapes which mark the landscape. The ancients of Bajor were gifted architects and engineers even while life on Earth was just entering the Stone Age.

The Bajoran system includes several planets, with Bajor the largest and most populous. Bajor has three moons and provides access to the only known "stable" wormhole, connecting the Alpha Quadrant with the Gamma Quadrant, tens of thousands of light years away. (First suggested in the NEXT GENERATION story "The Price.")

But Bajor is a world of contradictions. Although ancient, it is not powerful. It did not develop the technologies which led to warp drive and the weapons that could thereafter be created, and so it could not stand up to the might of the Cardassians when they arrived. Instead the Bajorans had turned inward, becoming a deeply mystical people with an ancient religion that bound them together as a people. They are a culture who believe in spiritual phenomena and are devoted to a non-secular philosophy that goes against the Federation's logical, scientific way of life. Their religious leader, known as the Kai, is curious and insightful and helped Commander Sisko when he first arrived on Deep Space Nine.

Due to the decades of conflict under the Cardassians, political factions have arisen. many of these factions have different views on what is best for Bajor, particularly now that it is rebuilding. Some look outwards to the promise of space and what the wormhole holds for them while others wish to return to the insular life they knew before the Cardassians came. This political situation remains precarious and the only stabilizing influence is the Kai, who remains honored and respected.

TERRORISTS WAIT AND WONDER

During the reign of the Cardassians, a terrorist underground had flourished, and Major Kira Nerys was a part of it. But like all terrorists, she found herself committing acts against the Cardassians which were just as revolting as the things that the Cardassians had committed against them. Eventually she found that she could not deal with this dichotomy and turned away from the terrorists. The terrorist underground still exists in scattered pockets, some on nearby worlds in the Bajoran system. The terrorists mistrust the motives of Starfleet and are willing to commit the same acts against them that they did against the Cardassians.

Although Major Kira is considered a turncoat by some in the underground, she depends on her old alliances to keep the terrorists largely in check so that Deep Space Nine does not erupt into a battleground between warring political factions. Thus far most of the underground has been willing to adopt a wait and see attitude regarding the

Federation. Since the provisional government of Bajor, which all political factions recognize, has requested admission into the Federation, the underground is willing to wait and see if Starfleet is as good as its word and will indeed protect and assist Bajor without dominating or otherwise attempting to unduly influence it.

This is a corner of the universe which has known war, suffering and deprivations of every sort. But some Bajorans who had escaped the domination of the Cardassians had already joined Starfleet in the hope of influencing the Federation into taking their up their cause. The fact that the Federation considered what was happening on Bajor as "an internal problem" did not go down well as the Bajorans considered the Prime Directive merely a tool which could be used against them by their oppressors. The Cardassians were able to so use it because they were not in the Federation, and neither was Bajor.

With Bajor abandoned by the Cardassians, and requesting admission to the Federation, they are finding that the Prime Directive can be invoked on their behalf as now any interference in their culture from another world would be considered a violation of the Prime Directive. They are not amused by the irony in that any more than they were when Bajoran refugee camps, which existed on several small worlds, would only be given humanitarian assistance by the Federation on a limited basis, i.e. food, clothing, medical supplies. "Just enough to keep us miserable," as one Bajoran remarked.

The resentment for the Federation's aloofness in the Bajoran's time of need will not be forgotten by many for a long time and so they feel that now it is the Federation and Starfleet who have something to prove to them. How Starfleet handles their stewardship aboard Deep Space Nine will determine how Bajor will respond to the rest of the Federation when the planet finishes rebuilding and takes their position with the other members of the Federation council.

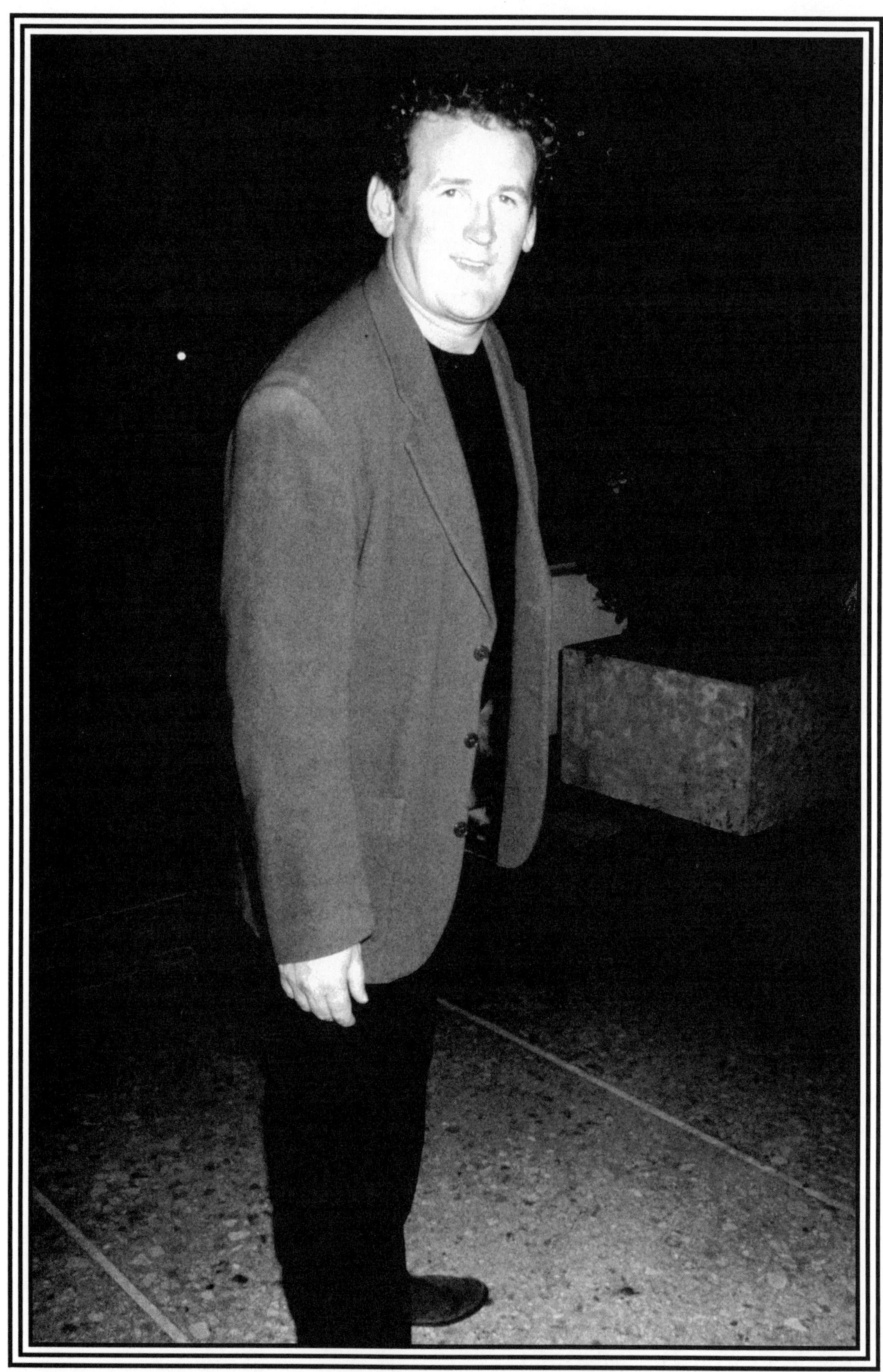

At the world premiere of the film HERO on September 21, 1992 in Century City, Colm Meaney turned out to see how his supporting role in this film turned out. ***Photo ©1993 Ortega/Ron Galella Ltd.***

STAR TREK—THE NEXT GENERATION—-DEEP SPACE NINE
Three series all set in the same universe and following a cohesive timeline. How do the main characters on these shows compare?

COMPARING TREKS

by Kay Doty

From the moment the news of a possible third STAR TREK series leaked to the public, fandom was a-buzz with rumors, guesses, speculation, and gossip. Objections came thick and fast. Many fans were aghast at the very thought of a STAR TREK without the Enterprise. How could a series be STAR TREK and not ". . . go where no one has gone before?" Did this mean the end of THE NEXT GENERATION? Fans wrote letters of protest, saying—We like what we have. In other words, "If it ain't broke, don't fix it."

Paramount, well aware that similar objections had surfaced when THE NEXT GENERATION was announced, and having watched the new series become a fan favorite and ratings winner, went ahead with their plans.

Executive Producers Rick Berman and Michael Piller put writers to work on scripts, and designers on drafting plans for the set, while they searched two continents for just the right actors. Hundreds were auditioned before the regulars were cast.

As with the casts of the preceding series, most of the selected actors and actresses were relatively unknown. Only Colm Meaney, who transferred from the Enterprise to Deep Space Nine, was well known to STAR TREK fans. Now, with the series midway through its first season, fans are accepting the new concept, and developing favorites from among the characters.

So how do they compare to their predecessors?

THE COMMANDING OFFICERS

Commander Benjamin Sisko (Avery Brooks) is a rank below the two ship's captains, James Kirk (William Shatner) and Jean-Luc Picard (Patrick Stewart), Sisko is an experienced Starfleet officer, and a veteran of the Wolf 359 massacre at the hands of the Borg. He is his own man and has his own method of command, but he also has some of the characteristics of both of his predecessors.

Sisko is not quite as likely to ". . . rush in where angels fear to tread," as Kirk did, nor does he call staff meetings, in the manner of Picard, to discuss an imminent crisis, an almost daily event on the space station.

Kirk commanded landing parties, something that Jean-Luc Picard has done much less frequently, due in part to a Command Directive that Captains can best serve by remaining aboard their ships. Sisko will, however, lead a foray into the wormhole if he feels he is the best man for the job, but he prefers to delegate authority. Like Kirk, he is inclined to make quick, on-his-feet decisions, and he expects them to be carried out immediately.

He has an office but spends much less time there than Picard spends in his ready room. Standing in the circle of the Operational Control Center, generally referred to as Ops, Sisko is surrounded by his senior officers, from whom he asks for reports and suggestions before making decisions.

Instead of the state-of-the-art ships that the captains enjoy, Sisko's command is a stationary space station located above Bajor in the far-reaches of Federation territory. Known as Deep Space Nine, the station was vandalized by Cardassians, the previous occupants, before their departure. Despite his crew's best efforts, there are usually more non-operational systems than those that are functional at any given time.

Explorers and protectors of Federation territory best describes what Kirk and Picard's positions are, but Sisko's is much more multi-faceted. Not only is he the Deep Space Nine commander, but first and foremost he is charged with preparing the Bajoran World for entry into the Federation. He must help them develop the newly discovered wormhole into a viable enterprise which will allow Bajor to restore their war-torn world. While Kirk and Picard went to seek out new life forms, Sisko waits for them to come to him.

Unlike Kirk and Picard, who never married, Sisko is a widower with a teenaged son. His wife, Jennifer, died at Wolf 359 three years prior to his taking command of Deep Space Nine. He is at last coming to terms with his grief over Jennifer's death and is determined to be as successful in his present post as Kirk and Picard have been in theirs.

THE FIRST OFFICERS

Commanders Spock (Leonard Nimoy) and William Riker (Jonathan Frakes), first officers under Kirk and Picard respectively, graduated from Starfleet Academy with high honors. Major Kira (Nana Visitor) Nerys's training came as a terrorist and freedom fighter who helped to free her world from the conquering Cardassians.

Spock and Riker have great respect and genuine affection for their commanding officers. It would not occur them, except under unusual circumstances, to question or disobey a direct order or go to a higher official. Sisko has earned Kira's grudging respect, but she isn't sure she likes him. She has questioned his orders, has disobeyed them, and gone over his head.

Kira doesn't want the Federation on the Space Station, but she has come to realize that if Bajor is ever to develop the wormhole and regain their independence, they must depend on Starfleet and the Federation for help. It is a constant irritant to Kira that Bajor doesn't have the capabilities for developing the wormhole's possibilities by themselves. This leaves her testy much of the time.

As time passes and Sisko convinces her that he does have the best interests of Bajor at heart, she will likely be a better first officer. However, if put to the test, and she must make a choice between Sisko and Bajor, it is very probable she would choose the latter. This would of needs be something more critical than just the support of one of her former comrades in the Bajoran terrorist movement as she has turned her back on those days and will not support such tactics used against the Federation.

CHIEF MEDICAL OFFICERS

When Doctors Leonard McCoy (DeForest Kelley), Beverly Crusher (Gates McFadden) and Katherine Pulaski (Diana Muldaur) first began their tours of duty on the Enterprise, their medical careers were well established. They were in their late thirties to early forties, and were considered among the best medical officers in Starfleet.

Lieutenant Julian Bashire CMO (Siddig El Fadil), newly graduated from Starfleet Medical Academy at age 26, was granted his request to be stationed on Deep Space Nine, possibly because not many doctors were anxious to spend a large chunk of their careers on the remote station. His youth gives him a naiveté and brashness the others have lost, but his skill as a physician is equal to that of his predecessors. In his specialty, alien anatomy, his knowledge and ability to diagnose and treat the non-human species he encounters is unmatched.

McCoy, Crusher, and Pulaski, despite their considerable skills have all agonized over the loss of an alien patient simply because they knew too little about the species to properly treat

them. As Bashir gains experience, it is very probable that he too will become one of Starfleet's most respected doctors.

While the Enterprise sickbays were the latest in modern technology, Bashir has to work in a facility which was stripped of many necessities by the departing Cardassians. His computers don't always work and his space is limited. But as hurriedly ordered state-of-the-art supplies arrive, it is safe to predict that Bashir's sickbay will be one of the show places on Deep Space Nine.

SCIENCE OFFICERS

It is interesting to note that Starfleet and the Federation seem to prefer non-humans as science officers in their most prestigious and/or important postings. Spock (Leonard Nimoy) was a Vulcan, Data is an android, and Lieutenant Jadzia Dax (Terry Farrel) is a Trill—a joined species that is two separate entities.

It is true that Spock was half-human, but he did everything within his power to subjugate that part of himself. He fought a frequently losing battle to suppress all emotion, and Data was not programmed with emotions. Dax, on the other hand, has over 300 years of emotions from other hosts to contend with. She is a new host to a symbiont that for over 50 years resided inside the body of a man. She is still struggling to separate her own emotions from those of the former host.

Dax is not the "computer" that Data is, nor has she reached the level of logic that Spock obtained, but her 350 years of real memories, plus her many science degrees, and her ability to manipulate a computer will put her on equal footing with Spock and Data.

CHIEF ENGINEER

Lt. Commander Montgomery Scott (James Doohan) earned a reputation as a miracle-worker by putting his beloved engines back together, usually under stressful conditions following a battle. Using the twenty-third century equivalent of baling wire, shoe-laces and glue, he frequently gave Captain Kirk that "little extra" to take them out of harm's way. Lt. Commander LaForge is equally ingenious at returning his damaged ship to operational status through the manipulation of his computers, clever use of the holodeck, and the ship's systems.

Chief Miles O'Brien (Colm Meaney) takes twenty-two years—five on the Enterprise 1704-D—of experience on starships with him to his new post as Chief of Operations on Deep Space Nine. After his promotion and transfer from the Enterprise to the Federation's most recently acquired space station, O'Brien soon realized that he'd be calling on every minute of that experience to keep the station up and running.

What he inherits is a vandalized station. Missing components are either damaged or destroyed. He doesn't always understand instructions that are written in the Bajoran or Cardassian languages. Nothing works, and when he gets a system up and running it doesn't always last. More times than he can count, his mind goes back to the pristine work areas of the Enterprise.

O'Brien fields more complaints than anyone else on the station, and despite his harried state of mind, somehow manages to handle each new crisis. His chief emotions are fatigue, and frustration. All of his problems aren't the result of the sabotaged station. His wife Keiko (Rosalind Chao) is not happy at leaving the Enterprise. She hates the deplorable conditions under which they and their three year-old daughter Molly, are forced to live. This creates friction between the couple—one problem that Scott and LaForge never encountered.

Despite his many problems, Commander Sisko and Starfleet Command are fully convinced that O'Brien is the man to bring order out of the chaos of Deep Space Nine.

CHIEF OF SECURITY

Like his counterparts on the Enterprise, Lieutenants Tasha Yar (Denise Crosby), and Worf (Michael Dorn), Constable Odo (Rene Auberjonois) is not a native of Earth. Odo is one of a kind, a shape-shifter who has no idea where his home world is, or who his people are. He was discovered alone in a space craft a half century earlier. The Bajorans raised him and accepted him without question. Odo had little, if any, training in the field of law enforcement. Like his friend Kira, he learned his craft while defending himself, and his adopted world, from the Cardassians.

Circumstances also forced Yar and Worf to spend their lives with people not of their own kind. Yar escaped from the rape gangs on her native planet, Hokma V, after her parents and most government officials were killed. Anarchists, who placed little value on the lives of others, became the rulers of her world.

Yar eventually overcame her fears and hatred enough to be accepted at Starfleet Academy. Upon graduation she was prompted by the horrors she had witnessed as a child, to become a security officer.

Worf's parents were also victims of war. His parents were killed by Romulans at the Battle of Khitomer. A Starfleet officer rescued him, and later, along with his wife, adopted the lonely child. Worf attended Starfleet Academy and became the first Klingon to serve as a Starfleet Officer. His warrior blood led him to become a security officer.

Odo, Worf and Yar, shared an ingrained belief in justice, but where Yar and Worf were quick to resort to phasers, Odo bars them from his domain. He does have one added advantage—his ability to change shape permits him to better keep ahead of the many, many crooks and criminals who

come his way. This ability is a shield against violent attacks.

HOSTESS/BARTENDER

Except that neither is human, there are few similarities between Quark (Armin Shimerman), the greedy owner/operator of the bar and gambling emporium on the Deep Space Nine promenade, and Guinan (Whoopi Goldberg), genial hostess of the Enterprise Ten-Forward lounge.

Quark, a Ferengi, is well endowed with his race's propensity for taking devious advantage of his fellow beings, if he can see a possibility for profit. Although he tries to keep his patrons under control, fights and loud disagreements are not uncommon. He is one of the least liked or trusted people on the station, and no one in their right mind would seriously consider confiding in him.

Guinan's origins are known only to her, the inhuman Q, and to a lessor degree, Picard. She runs Ten-Forward with grace and dignity, but is quick to spot, and just as quickly subdue trouble. She has the well known bartender's knack of listening to her customer's problems, frequently helping them find a solution. The antithesis of Quark, Guinan is one of the most popular beings on the Enterprise.

KIDS

Jake Sisko (Cirroc Lofton) is approximately the same age that Wesley Crusher (Wil Wheaton) was when he accompanied his mother, Dr. Beverly Crusher, aboard the Enterprise after she became the ship's CMO. Both are half orphans being raised by a single parent. Wesley's father and Jake's mother were killed in the line of duty.

Wesley is a genius whose ability earned him a field promotion to the rank of Ensign before he attended Starfleet Academy. His goal is to eventually become a ship's captain. Jake is bright, but not too happy about living in space. He is an obedient young man, but while Wesley was learning to become a Starfleet officer at the same age, Jake's boredom will occasionally lead him into trouble, especially when he teams up with Nog, Quark's nephew.

Quark's nephew was caught attempting to steal ore samples just minutes after Sisko assumed command of the space station. At the urging of Keiko O'Brien, Quark grudgingly enrolled the boy in her new school, ". . . for a few weeks to see how it works." He is a Ferengi, and the only reason Quark allowed him to attend was his own secret hope that school might teach the boy to be a smoother con-artist than his father. He may, at times, be a bad influence on Jake, but it is very probable that Jake's honesty will be a good influence on Nog. A typical relationship between teenagers that hasn't changed much over the centuries.

Although initially Nog seemed to be the controlling member of the duo, influencing Jake in some negative ways,

Jake Sisko has taken a stand amid refuses to let Nog push him into doing what he knows is wrong. In fact, when Nog's father pulled the Ferengi boy out of school because of the negative influence of the Nagus (a Ferengi leader), Jake secretly began to tutor Nog. The boy recognized his ignorance in important areas and didn't want to be the intellectual inferior of his friend and those he deals with.

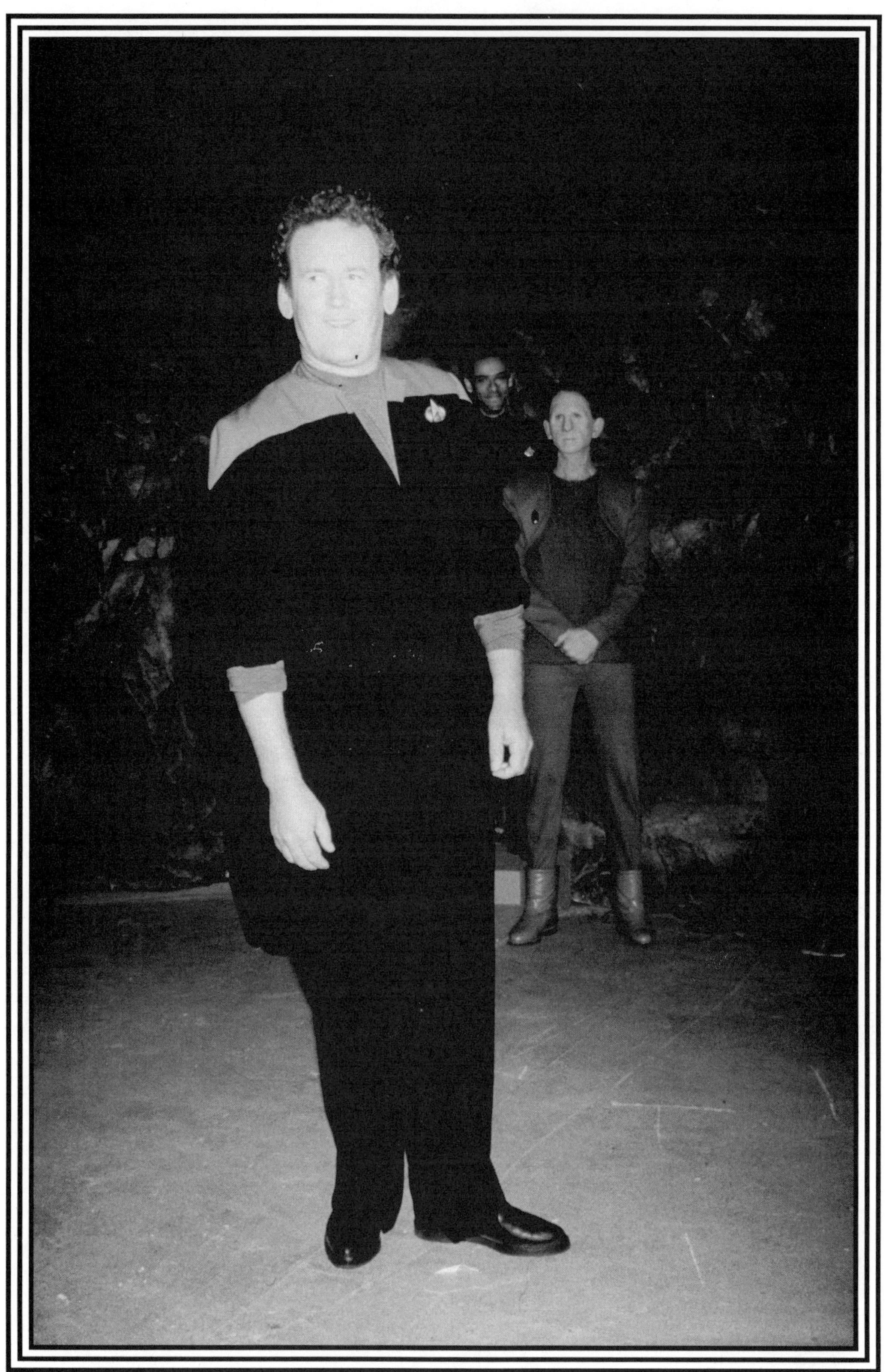

British actor Colm Meaney started out as a minor player on THE NEXT GENERATION but as Miles O'Brien he has received a promotion to featured player status on DEEP SPACE NINE.

THE CREW FROM DEEP SPACE

TREK: DEEPSPACE NINE

Siddig El Fadil with his fellow cast members. From left, Rick Berman (co-creator of DEEP SPACE NINE), Nana Visitor, Colm Meaney, Terry Farrell, Cirroc Lofton, Avery Brooks, Armin Shimerman, Rene Auberjonois, Siddig El Fadil, and Michael Piller (co-creator).

DOCTOR JULIAN BASHIR

by Kay Doty

Julian Bashir can't remember a time when he didn't want to be a doctor. His father was wealthy and could afford to educate his son in any profession that he chose. The boy chose medicine and never wavered.

Unlike so many children whose intellect is at or near genius level, Julian was a sociable child. But he had a tendency to chose his friends from among the offspring of doctors and scientists. He loved games, but not being particularly good at them, he was usually one of the first to be eliminated from competition.

When this occurred, Julian would seek out his host's library and immerse himself in whatever medical and/or science tapes, journals and books he might find there. Having tucked himself into a quiet corner or an isolated sofa to study his find, he was frequently an unseen listener to the conversations of his elders who might gather there.

This secret was first discovered when his friend's father and two colleagues were discussing a new technique that Julian had recently read about. His eagerness to learn more about the procedure was his undoing. Momentarily forgetting his status as an eavesdropper, he unwound himself from his hideaway in the folds of a deep chair, a series of questions tumbling from his lips.

The doctor's initial irritation at the boy's presence was soon allayed by the considerable knowledge, indicated by his questions, that he had gained on his own. His enthusiasm to learn and ability to absorb highly technical information earned him the privilege of sitting in on the doctors informal gatherings at social functions.

"Well, I wasn't exactly invited," Julian would explain years later, "but they didn't kick me out when I joined them."

He was frequently told he could stay only if he was quiet and didn't interrupt. This was often difficult for the boy who had many questions, but he did as he was told, enjoying what were some of the happiest moments of his young life.

Julian made his first discovery of the inter-workings of an emergency medical center by accident. He was twelve when a friend was injured in one of their ballgames and he helped carry the boy to a nearby center for treatment.

Julian was enthralled from the moment he walked through the door. He instantly loved the smell of the center, the professionalism of the medical staff, and the array of equipment that was visible from his seat in the waiting room. While he waited he helped dispel his teammates fears about their friend. Later when a young couple came in with a sick baby, he somewhat allayed the parents' fears by assuring them of the excellence of the staff. Their concern for their child was too great to wonder at the comfort being offered by one so young.

Julian had made a wonderful new discovery during his visit to the center. He began frequenting the facility, his eyes filled with wonder at seeing all the fantastic things he had only studied about. At first the staff considered him a nuisance and ordered him to leave, but he could no more stay away than he could go without eating.

He made himself useful by tidying the waiting room, getting drinks for people, and making calls to worried relatives of sick and injured patients. He was careful not to interfere with the staff as they went about their duties. After a time they accepted him and even asked him to do small tasks for them.

MOMENT OF TRUTH

The highlight of his pre-teen life occurred when an explosion filled the medical center with an overflow of seriously injured people. When he heard a doctor call repeatedly for a nurse, who were all occupied, Julian offered to help.

"Get scrubbed, then get back here and assist me," the doctor barked.

Julian didn't have to be told twice, and he was back at the doctor's side in minutes. His impromptu assignment included handing instruments to the doctor, moving gurneys carrying treated patients out of the operating area to make room for the next one needing treatment, and sponging perspiration from the doctor's face. The memory of the one task that would remain with him for the balance of his life was of gently covering the face of a young girl who had did not survive.

Nearly six hours passed before the last patient had been treated and removed from the emergency area. Fatigue dulled his expressive eyes and draped a gray pallor over his face as Julian and the exhausted medics collapsed in the staff lounge. The doctor who had put Julian to work studied the dark-haired youth, still clad in his green, several-sizes-too-large, blood-soaked surgery gown.

"Young man," the doctor spoke softly after studying the boy for several moments, "I would have lost at least two of those people if you hadn't been there to help me. You saved their lives. All of us owe you a debt of gratitude. Don't ever give up your dream to become a doctor."

"I won't, sir," the boy replied quietly, too tired to say more, but the sunshine of his smile drove the fatigue from his eyes, and the gloom from the lounge.

It wasn't until he was a teenager that Julian made the decision to practice space-medicine. He had visited the Lunar Recreational facilities on the moon countless times, but it wasn't until his parents took him on an extended tour of Earth's neighbors in the galaxy that Julian began his love affair with the stars.

The first stop on their odyssey into outer space was a visit to the Mars shipbuilding yard where his father had business interests. His mother's plans did not include Julian, so he went to his favorite tourist attraction—the base sickbay. He'd had the foresight to obtain a letter of introduction to the Mars Chief Medical Officer from one of the doctors at the medical center, thus when he presented himself at the front desk, he was granted a tour of the facility.

ALIEN SPECIALIST

Julian was so impressed that he knew in his heart, space was where he wanted to practice medicine. In addition to that decision, he was so fascinated with the wide variety of aliens he encountered, that he determined his studies would include as many alien life-form courses as the Starfleet Medical Academy had to offer.

Being Julian, he didn't wait until he entered the Academy to begin his study of aliens. This was a whole new world of medicine that he hadn't previously considered, but by the time he walked into the Academy as a lowly first-year student, he knew more about the anatomy of many of the alien beings in the galaxy than most of his classmates would know when they graduated.

Some of Julian's favorite texts were written by such doctors and scientists as the legendary Admiral Leonard McCoy, whose career covered nearly thirty years on two of the Enterprise starships; Zefram Cochrane inventor of the warp drive formula, and such Vulcan healers as Commander Selar.

With all of his advanced knowledge, Julian could have challenged numerous courses and finished in far less than the usual eight years. Fearing he might miss vital information by skipping classes, Julian spent the allotted time in training, but his early studies helped him to complete his Academy classes in record time, thus allowing him plenty of opportunity to pursue his considerable interest in members of the opposite gender.

Nor did he want for female companionship. His dark good looks, ready smile and charming personality assured him of that. And while he didn't exactly leave a trail of broken hearts, there were a few who deeply regretted their parting when he moved on. Julian looked at life as a great adventure, and he was not ready to dull his excitement at seeing the beckoning universe by making encumbering commitments.

Julian graduated second in his class. He missed just one question on the oral examination, or he would have been class valedictorian. He was actively sought after for a variety of positions on numerous ships, but the post he wanted wasn't on a ship. It was on a space station at the edge of Federation territory.

Through all his travels, his studies, and his knowledge of the surrounding galaxies, Julian never lost his love of adventure. When he arrived at Deep Space Nine, he brought with him a naiveté that is the bane of his more experienced fellow officers.

The thought of encountering spies, criminals, and other disreputable characters excites him. The new doctor is sometimes inclined to be innocently arrogant. He is an excellent doctor, knows it, and sees no reason to hide his light under a barrel. The one thing that transcends his normal genial good nature is the lack of proper fixtures and supplies in his sickbay. He believes every being has a right to the best care that he can provide, and until Starfleet and the Federation send him the latest equipment, he is not certain he can always give that care.

One of the most pleasant features of his posting on Deep Space Nine is the beautiful Science officer, Lieutenant Jadzia Dax. He knows she is a Trill and is host to a symbiont, but that just piques his interest. She does not return his ardor, making her even more desirable to him. Meanwhile his healthy libido doesn't prevent him from observing other fascinating females who frequent the station.

Dr. Julian Bashir arrived on the station with stars in his eyes, searching for adventure and ready to gallop into places where hardened space veterans know better than to go. In the meantime it did not take his fellow officers long to realize that Starfleet sent them one of the brightest doctors to come out of the Academy in a long time.

THE ACTOR: SIDDIG EL FADIL

Siddig's parents were living in the Sudan at the time of his birth. They left Africa to return to their native England when he was less than a year old. He was educated in the usual English public schools including a year at University College in London.

He worked two years in a men's clothing store. He quit the store and enrolled in an acting school, believing that would be the best way to learn to direct. He became a student at the London Academy of Music and Dramatic Arts (LAMDA) and appeared as the lead in such productions as "Hamlet" and "Arthur." Upon completion of the three year program at LAMDA, he joined the Manchester Library Theater in London where he appeared in the productions of "Brother Eichemann" and "Sinbad the Sailor."

After being cast in several minor stage roles, he became bored and swore that he'd never act again. But never is a long time, especially for a broke, out-of-work former actor, and would-be director. He finally got to try his hand at directing at the Arts Threshold Theatre with the productions of "Lotus and the Rats" and "Julius Caesar." It was while he was working there as a director that he secured an acting role on television. He was offered a role in a six-part mini-series, BIG BATTALIONS, in which he played a Palestinian. He accepted the part and made his television debut in 1991.

A fine performance in the mini-series led to the role of King Faisel in A DANGEROUS MAN—LAWRENCE AFTER ARABIA, and that led to Dr. Bashir in DEEP SPACE NINE. Siddig El Fadil was cast in the role of DEEP SPACE NINE's Doctor Julian Bashir almost by a fluke. PBS stations carried the British-made film, in which El Fadil played King Faisel, but it was a minor role. The made-for-TV movie didn't attract much of the viewing public, but one who did see the show was Rick Berman, co-executive producer of DEEP SPACE NINE.

As King Faisal in this British television drama about T.E. Lawrence (of Arabia, that is), El Fadil was made up to portray a man much older than himself, and Piller and Berman were so impressed by his performance as the King that they seriously thought about trying him out for the role of another leader, Commander Sisko. When Paramount's representatives in Great Britain tracked El Fadil down in London, they relayed some surprising information to Rick Berman: El Fadil was only in his mid-twenties, a bit younger than the actor they hoped to find for the role of Sisko! On the other hand, it would obviously have been a great mistake to

pass up an opportunity to employ an actor as good as El Fadil, so they had him read for the part of the young medical officer.

Berman had been quite impressed with El Fadil's performance, stating, "He just blew me away." The people at Paramount liked what they saw and invited the young actor to come to the States for further testing. Everyone thought he was wonderful, ending their search for the space station doctor. He was originally auditioned for the part of Benjamin Sisko, but it was thought that at 24, he was too young for the lead. Even as the doctor, he is supposed to be 27.

Berman and co-producer Michael Piller had not envisioned a doctor with a British accent, but the actor's versatility and fresh look made him their first, and only, choice. Paramount officials believe that these attributes, along with his dark good looks and personable demeanor will soon make him a fan favorite.

Indeed, at this writing only nine episodes, in addition to the two-hour premiere, have aired, but already he is beginning to receive fan mail. This comes as something of a shock to El Fadil who said that people in England don't write letters to people they don't know.

El Fadil, who is single, says he may go back to London during hiatus, but is happily exploring as much of America as his ten to sixteen hour work days will allow. He lives in West Hollywood, is beginning to make friends away from the studio, and enjoying life in a way that a year ago he would have said was impossible. A wide smile lights up his face when he talks about a long run with DEEP SPACE NINE and the STAR TREK universe, but insists he is more interested in the present, and believes the future will take care of itself.

LT. JADZIA DAX

Dax is a member of a joined species known as the Trill. She combines the host body of a 28 year old female with an ancient creature who survives into its seventh lifetime. The symbiotic relationship is extremely complex. Jadzia shares Dax's wisdom and experience and can recall all his memories over more than three hundred years. Dax has been a mother three times and a father twice. Its last host was Curzon Dax, who served as Sisko's mentor. Benjamin was Curzon Dax's friend for nearly twenty years.

A Trill is comprised of two separate but interdependent entities: a host and a symbiont. The host provides a humanoid body. The symbiont is an invertebrate, androgynous lifeform that lives within the host. It looks like a short, fat snake. Centuries ago the symbionts lived underground while the humanoids thrived on the surface of their world. But due to an environmental disaster, they were forced to unite in order to survive. As time went on this mutual support evolved into a biological interdependency and thus two individuals became one. They speak with one voice (you can't ask to speak with the symbiont or the host, only the combined lifeform). The symbiont's life span is much longer than that of the host body, and as a result one symbiont will be combined with several hosts during its life.

Dax was implanted into Jadzia's body when Curzon died. Jadzia relived the incident during her research on the Bajoran orbs. When a host dies, doctors surgically remove the symbiont. The worm then burrows itself into the new host. Dax's host was joined with her symbiont when she was an adult. The symbiont part of her is three hundred years old, and is a brilliant scientist with an innate wisdom who can draw upon a library of knowledge built from six lifetimes of experience.

Jadzia trained long and hard to pass the various mental, physical and psychological testing required to serve as host—the highest honor her people can receive. Jadzia was quite the academician and scholar, with doctorates in several separate scientific disciplines including premiere distinctions in exobiology, zoology, astrophysics and exoarcheology. She earned all of these degrees as Jadzia, before being joined with Dax.

Jadzia wanted to be a Trill host since childhood. She won many scholarships and competed in competition with other young Trill candidates. Jadzia excelled in all character profiles as well. Both personalities are blended together. Neither is suppressed. Jadzia Dax made legal history when an attempt was made to prosecute Dax for crimes that Curzon Dax was accused of, including treason and the assassination of General Tundro. Trill Minister Selar Peers testified in the extradition hearing. Dr. Bashir explained how the symbiont and host are biologically interdependent. Ninety-three hours after they are joined, neither can survive without the other.

The result of the joining is a serene character who brings a calm, centered voice to any discussion; patient, confident and wise. Dax could be thought of as something like an ancient Zen master in the body of a twenty-eight year old woman. There is a subtle conflict within her, a generation gap of sorts. The older symbiont suppresses the youthful instincts of the host. And so, sometimes she will seem controlled when a part of her really would like to let go. For example, the three hundred year old worm has no use for sex or passion except as it serves procreation, but occasionally the youthful instincts of the host overcomes that resistance, as revealed in the episode appropriately titled "Dax."

In that episode, when Dax was accused of causing the death of a famous general thirty years before, she had to appear at an extradition hearing, which also examined the nature of Trills and whether a new host body could be subjected to punishment for what a previous host body had done. Dr. Bashir explained at the hearing that the brain waves are different for the host and the symbiont. Two brains, like two computers linked together, operate with two distinct patterns, even if they operate simultaneously. Curzon Dax and Jadzia Dax are as different as night and day. Curzon was a hard-drinking womanizer. Jadzia is a young, studious woman.

Curzon Dax was exonerated after the late general's widow gave Dax the embarrassing alibi, that Curzon was in her bed when the general himself betrayed the cause and was slain by the rebels. Jadzia Dax was willing to sacrifice herself to protect Anina Tundro, whom Curzon Dax had loved. Jadzia also acted to protect her species as a whole, as well as to preserve the honored memory of the general.

Dax and Ben Sisko have worked together before as Curzon Dax was Ben Sisko's mentor years before. The only trouble is that back then, Dax was still in the host body of an elderly man. Her sexually attractive new form creates a certain amount of unspoken tension between her and Sisko, which they both resist. After all, he's still having a hard time getting used to the fact that she's a three hundred year old worm, but he doesn't hide the respect and affection he has for her.

Julian Bashir, even though he understands perfectly the symbiotic relationship of a Trill, is still very much attracted to Jadzia Dax and imagines that he can, perhaps, get her to respond to him.

THE ACTOR: TERRY FARRELL

The role of Jadzia Dax went through a number of drastic changes during the pre-production work on DEEP SPACE NINE. As originally conceived, Dax was to have been a character from an alien world who, due to differences in the relative gravity of DS9 and her home planet, would require a high-tech wheelchair in order to function outside of her special office. (This is what is referred to in the Twenty-Fourth Century as being "gravitationally challenged.") When this notion was thought through, it was seen to present considerable production challenges, and so the original idea was scrapped, and Piller and Berman cast around for another alien until they hit upon the Trill, a symbiotic race that had been introduced in the Rene Echevarria scripted NEXT GENERATION episode, "The Host".

With all these eleventh hour alterations, Terry Farrell (who the producers spotted in the horror turkey HELLRAISER III) became the last member of the regular DEEP SPACE NINE cast to be signed on. Only one among many talented and beautiful young women trying out for the role, Farrell landed the part of Dax because she was seemed to understand the concept behind the character. Some of the actresses, trying to grasp the symbionic concept, thought that it would be a good idea to pitch their voices like a man's—not what the creators of the show had in mind. Farrell grasped the concept of an extremely old, wise mind looking at the world through the eyes of a beautiful young person. A character who would, after all, be somewhat bemused by the attentions inspired by her outward physical form after having changed bodies any number of times during the past four centuries.

Terry Farrell began shooting her first scenes for the DEEP SPACE NINE pilot in full Trill make-up. Paramount Studio executives, seeing her in that make-up, reacted negatively. They didn't like the notion that this beautiful young actress had her features obscured beneath heavy make-up. Two days worth of footage were scrapped, and make-up wizard Michael Westmore had to come up with a quick

replacement design. He came up with a subtle spotting around the sides of the face that enhanced Terry Farrell's natural features rather than concealing them.

Terry Farrell was born in Cedar Rapids, Iowa and at the age of 16 signed with the prestigious Elite modeling agency and moved to New York City. For several years she worked as a model, appearing on the cover of such magazines as VOGUE and MADEMOISELLE.

She got her television start in the short-lived 1984 ABC series PAPER DOLLS (with Jonathan Frakes as a co-star), portraying the "smart" model Laurie Caswell. She also appeared in an episode of the new TWILIGHT ZONE. (In a remake of "After Hours" she plays the Anne Francis role of a mannequin which comes to life in a department store.)

Terry also had a guest appearance on QUANTUM LEAP ("Leap For Lisa," in which she plays a nurse that was the love of Dean Stockwell's character when he was in the Navy. Scott Bakula's character jumps into Dean's character's body as he is accused of killing the nurse.) She's also appeared in guest star roles on THE COSBY SHOW and FAMILY TIES.

Her film credits include Rodney Dangerfield's BACK TO SCHOOL and BEVERLY HILLS MADAM with Faye Dunaway. She played a victim of serial killer Ted Bundy in the film DELIBERATE STRANGER with Mark Harmon, and recently co-starred in HELLRAISER III: HELL ON EARTH as a reporter. She is now a resident of Los Angeles where she lives with her dog, Freckles.

Farrell was the last actor cast for DEEP SPACE NINE. Farrel read for the part on the NEXT GENERATION set and "survived the technobabble," as she put it. Farrell was quoted in STARLOG magazine on Jadzia's sex life by stating—"Dax would say, 'Hey! Sex is just for procreation.' Though after three hundred years, I would imagine I'm pretty good at it." She was also quoted about being thrilled to get the job as Dax since she was such a STAR TREK fan: "I was freaking out! I said, 'I used to watch STAR TREK when I was a little girl,' my grandma made me a Tribble once. It was just too weird."

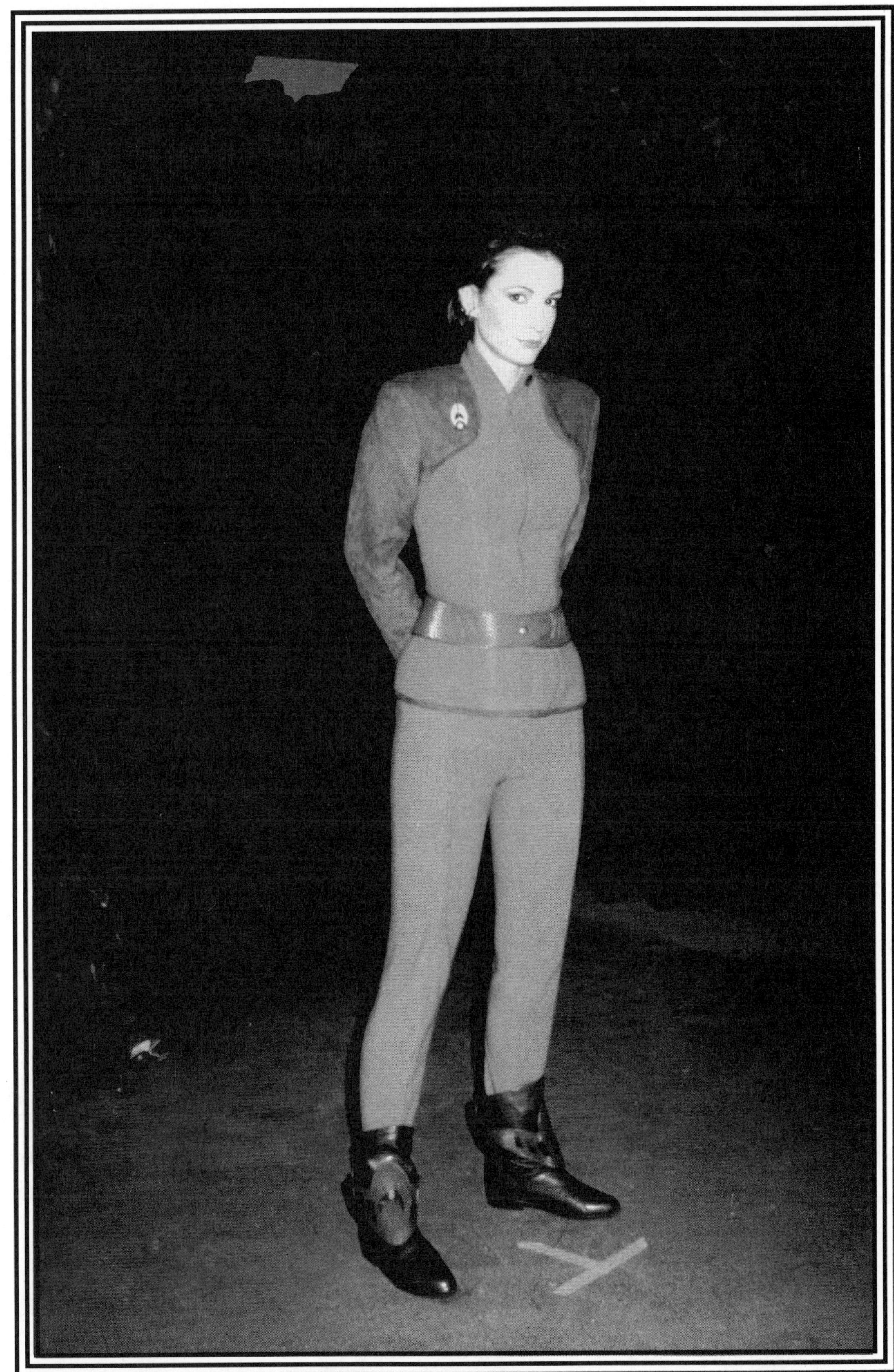

Nana Visitor, who plays Major Kira Nerys on DEEP SPACE NINE.

Photo ©1993 Ortega/Ron Galella Ltd.

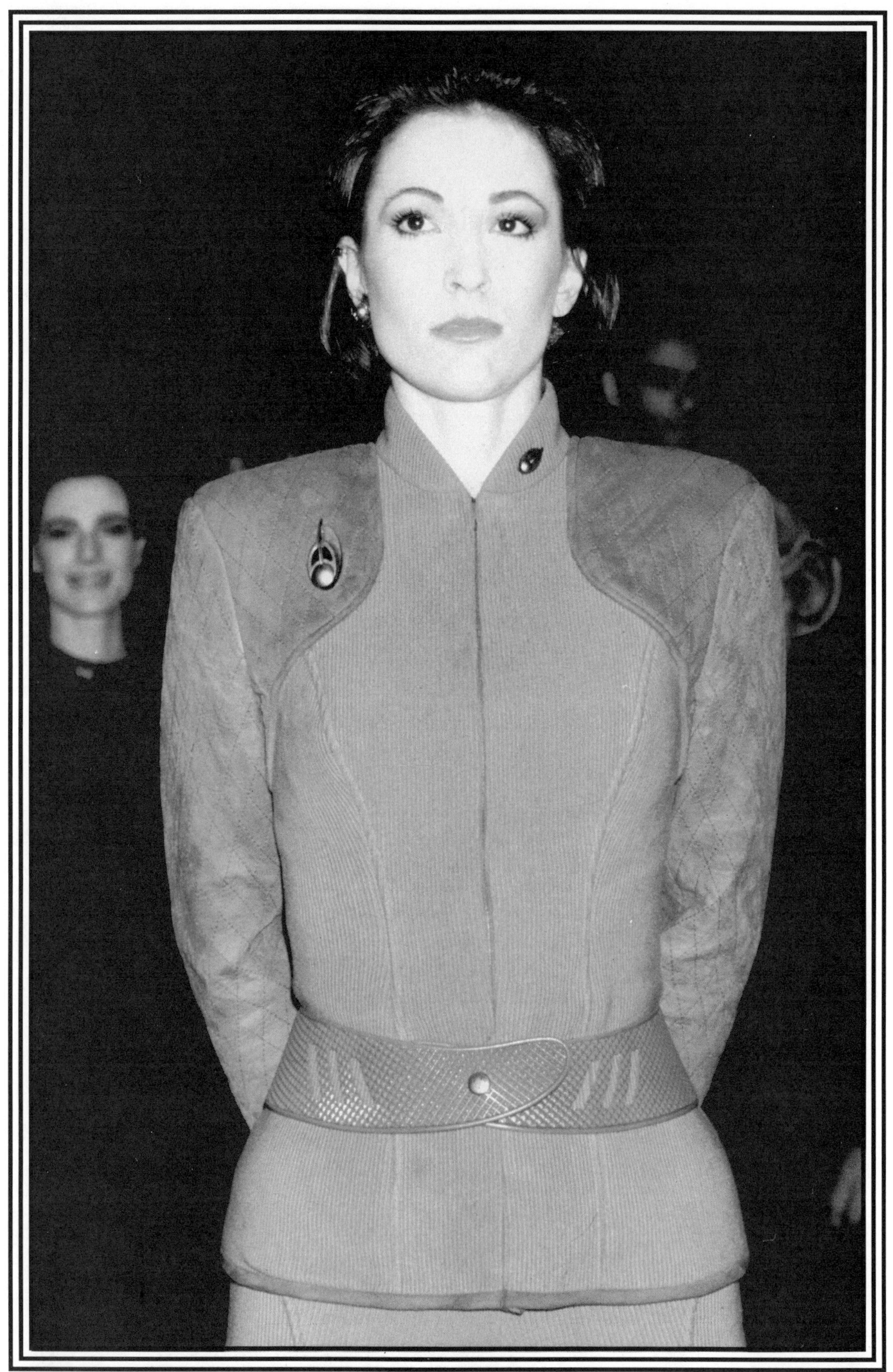

Nana Visitor, who plays Nerys, at the DEEP SPACE NINE press conference held September 2, 1992.

Photo ©1993 Ortega/Ron Galella Ltd.

MAJOR KIRA NEYRS

by Alex Burleson

Kira Neyrs grew up fighting the ruthless Cardassian overlords on her home planet of Bajor and became a terrorist to help win independence. She is a former major in the Bajoran underground. She finally quit the organization after finding out what tactics they used, up to and including chemical biological warfare. She proved her loyalty to the Federation when she destroyed an explosive which had been designed to destroy the wormhole. Having fought for freedom all her life, it has angered her to see the older leaders throw it away through their petty dissensions. She tried without success to reach the Kai herself to air her grievances. It's very possible that she was sent by the government to be the Bajoran administrator at the station simply to get her outspoken voice out of earshot.

At first, Kira was not a supporter of Federation involvement at Deep Space Nine, preferring that Bajor remain independent of all outside interests. She initially viewed the Federation arrival with suspicion, as it seemed that the Bajor were exchanging one powerful overlord for another. As the representative of the Bajorans on board the space station, she has no confidence in Sisko when he arrives. In fact she's working in his office when he gets there, clearly having taken charge. She steps down from that position with ill-disguised reluctance.

She considers herself an administrator more than an adventurer, but proves her worth at Red Alert, and once even tried to hold off an entire Cardassian fleet in the unarmed space station. Sisko's arrival with a Cardassian warship in a Runabout's tractor-beam took the fight out of the fleet and saved Kira from the humiliation she would have born in surrender. She also learned not to try to go over Sisko's head (Even if it is to Spock's wife—Susan Bay). Major Kira (Bajorans family name is first) is proud of Bajor.

Kira loathes the Cardassians and she committed atrocities against them in the name of freedom, some of which bother her now. When others in the Bajoran underground begin a new wave of terrorism, she is forced into a moral quandary about tracking them down and bringing them to justice. Former terrorists consider her a turncoat because she won't join with them in violently opposing the presence of the Federation on Bajor. Kira will come to respect and bond with Sisko, although they will continue to have different agendas as new issues arise.

THE ACTOR: NANA VISITOR

Nana Visitor was born and raised in New York City on the west side, in and around the theater district where her father was a successful choreographer on Broadway. Her mother ran a dance studio and was a ballet teacher. So her interest in performing was clearly in the blood. At age seven, Nana began to study ballet at her mother's studio.

Following high school graduation, Nana began appearing on the legitimate stage in such productions as "42nd Street," "Gypsy," (with Angela Lansbury) and "My One And Only," "The Ladies Room" at the Tiffany Theater in Los Angeles and "A Musical Jubilee." While still living in New York she also secured regular roles on the daytime dramas ONE LIFE TO LIVE and RYAN'S HOPE. She had an early movie role in the 1977 film THE SENTINEL, a horror movie based on a bestseller.

While working as a fledgling actress she was also employed as a dancer although becoming a successful actress was always her first goal. She pursued this seriously by relocating from New York to Los Angeles in 1985. Soon after she found guest star roles on such TV shows as JAKE AND THE FATMAN, BABY TALK, MURDER SHE WROTE, L.A. LAW, EMPTY NEST, IN THE HEAT OF THE NIGHT, MATLOCK and THIRTYSOMETHING. She also had the supporting role of Bryn Newhouse on the short-lived NBC television series WORKING GIRL.

While growing up in New York, Nana Visitor watched reruns of the original STAR TREK every day at six o'clock. What she felt made the original series work were the relationships and this is what she feels will also be a strong point of DEEP SPACE NINE. The actress feels that the reason that Major Kira and Jadzia Dax were made such strong characters was in response to the constant lobbying of Marina Sirtis on THE NEXT GENERATION to make female characters stronger and less traditional on that show. While Berman and Piller could only change things to a degree on THE NEXT GENERATION, since that show was created by Gene Roddenberry, the possibilities were wide open on DEEP SPACE NINE when it came to the characterizations.

Nana Visitor is looking forward to a long run on the series and appreciates the opportunity the series offers due to how difficult it is for actors to find work in the very competitive film and television industry. “To be working is great, period,” The actress told STARLOG. “There are so many actresses my age who aren’t working. They’re really talented, really beautiful. I’m just thrilled and grateful to be working, and to be working on STAR TREK. We’re part of the futurists’ thoughts and ideas. Many people are putting a lot of creativity, effort, care and love into this show every day, so I’m really looking forward to the experience that’s ahead of all of us.”

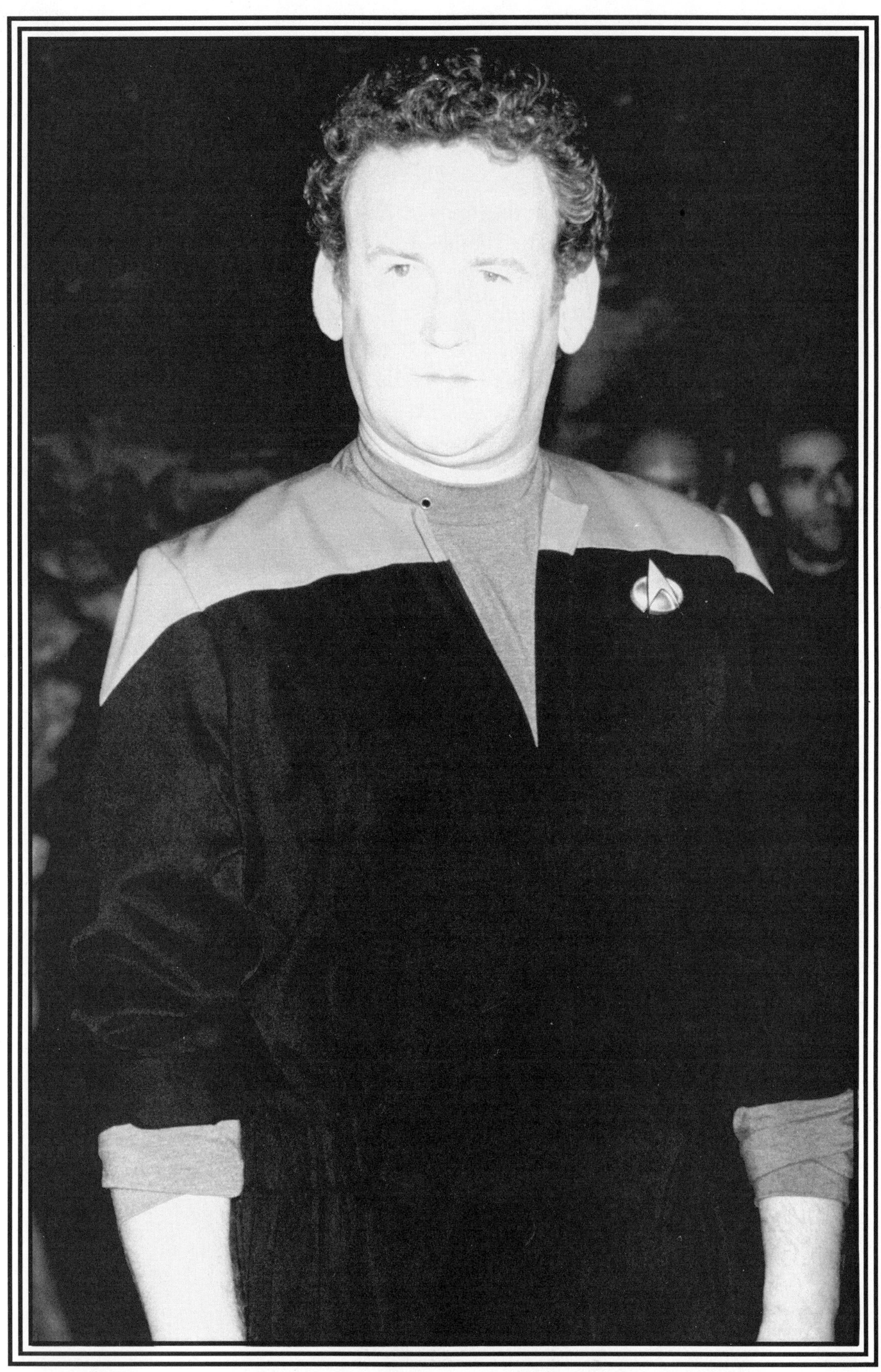

Colm Meaney, who originated the role of Miles O'Brien on STAR TREK: THE NEXT GENERATION, reprises the part on DEEP SPACE NINE. *Photo ©1993 Ortega/Ron Galella Ltd.*

CHIEF OPERATIONS OFFICER MILES O'BRIEN

by Kay Doty

Graduating fourth in his class, Miles O'Brien applied for, and was given, an assignment in deep space. His first ship was a small passenger liner, an assignment that gave him ample opportunity to hone his transporter skills. He didn't however get as deep into space as he would have liked. That came several years later when he transferred to the USS Rutledge under the command of Captain Benjamin Maxwell.

O'Brien, a likable, jovial man with a quick wit and ready smile, has a talent at repairing any malfunction. The captain observed the young technician for several months before promoting him to the post of Bridge Tactical Officer, with the rank of Lieutenant j.g.

While serving on the Rutledge, the ship was ordered to Selik 3 where an outpost was under attack by Cardassian marauders. O'Brien was a member of the party sent into defend the residents, but the Rutledge had arrived too late. Over a hundred people at the outpost, including Captain Maxwell's wife and children, had been murdered.

During hand-to-hand combat with two of the raiders, O'Brien stunned one and killed the other. He had never previously been forced to kill anyone and he was profoundly shaken by the incident. He'd been forced to take a life and witnessed the worst sort of butchery of innocent civilians performed by the ruthless marauders. O'Brien was left with a deep-seated resentment of all Cardassians.

Soon after the Selik 3 incident, O'Brien earned the rank of full lieutenant and transferred to the USS Enterprise under the command of Captain Jean Luc Picard.

Lt. O'Brien served at various posts including bridge conn officer and transporter technician, and occasionally filling in as a security officer. A couple of years after O'Brien joined the Enterprise, Geordi LaForge, who had been responsible for overseeing the transporter operation, became the chief engineer with the rank of Lt. Commander. He immediately recommended that O'Brien become the new transporter chief.

The arrangement worked well, for not only was the new transporter chief one of the most knowledgeable in Starfleet, but his congenial personality made him a favorite of officers and crew alike.

O'Brien has two passions; his love of women and gambling, not necessarily in that order. After joining the Enterprise, word of his skill with a deck of cards earned him an invitation to join the officer's weekly poker game.

If O'Brien had visions of cleaning out his fellow officers credit accounts (and he did), his plans received a jolt in the person of the ship's first officer, Commander William Riker. Riker and O'Brien were both shrewd masters of the game and equally adept at bluffing. There were times when their fellow players threw in their cards and watched while the two went head to head. By the end of the first session in which O'Brien participated, no one, including Riker, considered him a patsy.

As the man most responsible for transporting people on and off of the ship, O'Brien was seldom part of an away team. His duties included the maintenance and operation of the ship's transporter systems—to have them ready for use at a moment's notice, and to be damned certain he didn't put anyone down inside a solid wall.

Therefore he was pleasantly surprised when Commander Riker included him in an away team that would be beaming to Alphard V—the best known gambling planet in the galaxy.

To date eighteen men, including Starfleet Captain Dale Robbins, had disappeared from Alphard V without a trace. No ransom demands issued, no bodies found, no prisoner exchange ultimatum. They were just gone.

Dressed in the latest civilian attire of wealthy tourists, O'Brien, Riker, Counselor Troi, and Lt. Worf, along with two female security guards, were bait for the kidnappers.

For a time it was a pleasant mission. O'Brien could gamble as much as he chose. In fact he was ordered to do so while using Federation credits. A very pretty security guard was his companion.

After the passage of three hours it became apparent that O'Brien had been selected as the next victim. This was where the kidnappers made their biggest mistake. Their ship's transporter was not functioning properly and they had inadvertently brought aboard the one man most qualified to use the problem to his advantage.

O'Brien and his companion, Ensign Jardenaux, had materialized near the overhead and been unceremoniously dumped to the deck several feet below. In the scuffle that followed, O'Brien managed to activate his communicator and summon the other members of the away team to the alien ship. In the ensuing battle O'Brien not only saved Jardenaux's life, but was able to direct the away team to the abductors' location and help recover the other victims and subdue their captors. Commander Riker recommended a commendation be placed in O'Brien's permanent file. But the transporter chief had one question—"Why me?"

"Because," Riker said with a grin, "of all the people on this ship you are the one I thought would be most convincing as a dedicated gambler, and least likely to be spotted as a plant."

On the opposite end of the pleasure scale was O'Brien's marriage to Keiko Ishikawa, the ship's botanist. With Geordi as his best man, Data filling in as the father of the bride, and Captain Picard officiating, the pretty Japanese/Irish ceremony was held in the specially decorated Ten Forward. The couple later became the parents of a daughter, Molly.

After serving 22 years aboard a variety of ships, O'Brien was again promoted, and accepted a transfer to Deep Space Nine as Chief Operations Officer. Keiko and their three year old daughter accompanied him.

Upon arriving at the space station, O'Brien found that it had been trashed by the Cardassians when they'd been forced to leave. This meant that all the electronics on the station had to be checked out and repaired. O'Brien proved he was up to the demands of his job.

His wife, Keiko, didn't embrace the new assignment as readily as Miles did. She found the adjustment a difficult one to make. But when she was able to establish a school for the children who live on DS9 she at last found a fulfilling role for herself.

Miles O'Brien has made important contributions to the running and operations of DS9, such as when he helped to find subspace shunts hidden by a criminal who was hiding on the station, as well as when he recognized Q as being present and reported the sighting to Commander Sisko.

THE ACTOR: COLM MEANEY

Meaney was born and raised in Dublin, Ireland and began acting at the age of 14. After finishing public school he applied for admittance to the Irish National Theater, part of the National Irish Theatre drama school. While waiting to be accepted he worked on a fishing boat. The day he was accepted at the school he gave up the professional fishing business forever. He spent eight years appearing in many theatrical productions in England, including "Accidental Death of an Anarchist" and "Fish in the Sea." It was then that Colm made his first television appearance in the BBC TV show "Z CARS" and the independent British production of STRANGERS before he relocated to New York.

A versatile actor who is seldom out of work, Meaney has portrayed a wide variety of roles on stage, big screen and television. He first came to the United States in 1978 and spent the next four years dividing his time between roles in London and New York before settling permanently in his adopted country. The next three or four years found him working in off-Broadway and regional theatre. His decision to move to Los Angeles in the mid 1980's brought a change to film and television.

On American television he appeared on various series in guest starring roles, including MOONLIGHTING, REMINGTON STEELE, TALES FROM THE DARK SIDE and in the pilot episode of the Jane Seymour series DR. QUINN, MEDICINE WOMAN.

Because of his accent, Meaney was frequently cast as a villain, but admits he likes the nice guy roles. As Chief O'Brien he has become a household name, at least among Star Trek fans, but despite appearing in nearly sixty episodes, he has not been type cast and continues to appear in other roles.

When Colm Meaney's agent suggested he audition for STAR TREK: THE NEXT GENERATION, the actor not only had never seen any of the original series episodes or movies, but he wasn't even a science fiction fan.

He read for several of the main roles, and while others were chosen for those, the powers-that-be liked Meaney well enough to find occasional spots to use him on the series during the first two seasons.

When Colm Meaney first came in to try out for STAR TREK: THE NEXT GENERATION, the producers were looking for someone to portray the role of Data;

obviously Meaney was passed over for this, but he was eventually cast in the part of a nameless Transporter technician in such early episodes as "Encounter At Farpoint" and "The Naked Now."

Meaney began his STAR TREK: THE NEXT GENERATION career as a bridge officer in the first three episodes of the series. Believing that he wouldn't be used again in the series, he returned to New York to do a play, "Breaking the Code," with Derek Jacobi. When "Code" closed a year later, the writer's strike was in progress and THE NEXT GENERATION was in limbo. He accepted a short-lived role on the daytime soap, ONE LIFE TO LIVE that lasted until the fall of 1988 and the end of the strike.

When the strike ended, Meaney was called back by Paramount to reprise his role as the character who, after four or five episodes, was given the name O'Brien. Beginning with the strike-shortened 1988/89 season, Meaney's character was given a regular job on the ship and appeared in seventeen episodes. In the fourth season episode "Family" he was given the full name, Miles Edward O'Brien.

The actor, who describes himself as an "irregular regular" has not appeared in as many episodes as viewers might believe. Frequently orders from the bridge to "Energize, Mr. O'Brien," continue the illusion that the actor is indeed in the episode. But unlike Lt. Kyle, his counterpart on the old Enterprise, Chief O'Brien has been featured prominently in several episodes.

One of these was the second season "Unnatural Selection" in which O'Brien was instrumental in reversing Dr. Pulaski's (Diana Muldaur) rapid aging by skillful use of the transporter. He was also featured in season four's "The Wounded," when O'Brien talks his former captain, turned renegade, into surrendering. Meaney even gets to sing a bit in this one.

A talented comic, Meaney enjoys adding a sense of humor to his character whenever possible.

The Irish actor has slowly been insinuating his presence into a number of movies in recent years: his big-screen appearances have included a part in Warren Beatty's DICK TRACY, his role as Dennis Quaid's brother in the Alan Parker film COME SEE THE PARADISE, the part of an airline captain in DIE HARD II: DIE HARDER, and as one of Tommy Lee Jones' villainous henchmen in the Steven Seagal action thriller UNDER SIEGE. He's also appeared in THE GAMBLER III, FAR AND AWAY with Tom Cruise, and THE LAST OF THE MOHICANS. Colm also appeared in the role of Jimmy Robert, Sr. in THE COMMITMENTS.

Meaney demonstrated his well developed ability at playing the villain in "Power Play" during the fifth season. In that episode he, Counselor Troi, and Data were possessed by criminals long held on the prison moon Mab-Bu Vi. The trio were excellent as they terrorized the ship's crew, while Meaney gave a chilling performance when he menaced his own wife and child.

The theme was again fear in "Realm of Fear" during the sixth season when O'Brien assisted Lieutenant Barkley to overcome his fear of the transporter, while explaining how he had conquered his own aversion to spiders.

Perhaps Meaney is best remembered by STAR TREK viewers when, in his role of O'Brien, he became the first regular Enterprise crew member to be married on screen. His beautiful bride, Keiko, was played by Rosalind Chao.

Fans have frequently asked about the similarities between Meaney and James Doohan (Scotty in the original series) and their STAR TREK roles. Both O'Brien and Doohan's Scotty are in engineering, and both characters are very good at their jobs. The similarities end there.

Doohan was, and is, well known for his ability to portray a variety of accents, while Meaney's accent is his own. Meaney hails from Ireland and Doohan was born in Canada. One thing the actors do have in common—both are well received guests at conventions.

As his presence on the series became more frequent, Colm Meaney's character began to take on a more prominent role, emerging as an important supporting character. When Rick Berman and Michael Piller began casting DEEP SPACE NINE, Meaney agreed to jump ship and become a regular on the new show. So now Meaney has moved on to the more crucial leading role as the Chief of Operations on the ramshackle space station, Deep Space Nine.

Meaney is married and has a pre-teenaged daughter, Brenda, who is an ardent fan of STAR TREK. He helped Tom Cruise with his Irish accent during FAR AND AWAY's filming. Meaney's wife Barbara and 8-year-old daughter, Brenda, often accompany him on location.

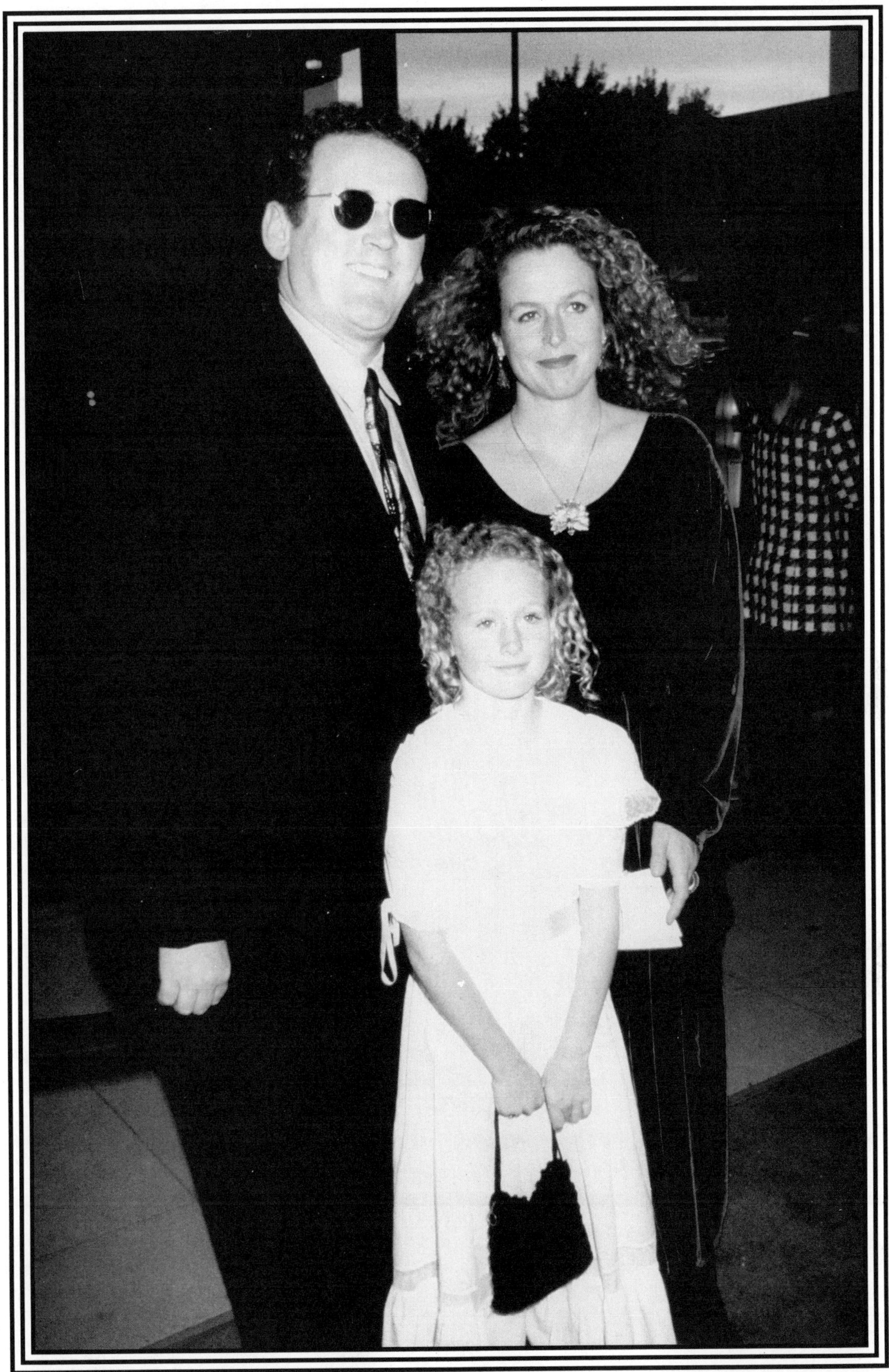

On May 20, 1992, Colm Meaney (Miles O'Brien) with wife Barbara and daughter Brenda appeared at the world premiere of the Tom Cruise film FAR AND AWAY. *Photo ©1993 Ortega/Ron Galella Ltd.*

At the DEEP SPACE NINE presentation where the cast met the press, Rene Auberjonois answered questions about the alien shape-shifter he plays on DEEP SPACE NINE. *Photo ©1993 Ortega/Ron Galella Ltd.*

SECURITY CHIEF ODO

Fifty years before the Federation came to Deep Space Nine, a spacecraft was found drifting not far from Bajor near the Denorios asteroid belt. Aboard it was an alien who had no memory of who he was nor where he was from. He came to be called Odo. Since he was found by the Bajor, he lived among them. At first he was sort of an 'elephant man,' a source of curiosity and humor as he turned himself into a chair or a pencil. Raised with no knowledge of his past or who he really is, Odo the shape-shifter chose to adopt a humanoid form to better relate with the races he grew up among.

Odo's true shape is that of a formless blob. He sleeps in a bucket at night as he must return to his true form once each day. Although he has adopted a humanoid shape, he resents it. As a result, Odo performs a uniquely important role in the ensemble of main characters. He is the character who explores and comments on human values. And because he is forced to pass as one of us, his point of view usually comes with a cynical edge.

With the Cardassians in charge on Bajor and in control of the station known as Deep Space Nine, Odo found himself having to associate with them. The more he got to know them the less he liked what he knew. But even the Cardassians needed people to keep the order and thus Odo secured the job of Chief of Security on Deep Space Nine. In the course of his duties he got to know the Ferengi, Quark, and learned that the Cardassians could have learned things about treachery from the Ferengi.

When the Bajorans overthrew the century of iron rule of the Cardassians Odo was determined to maintain order and kept the station from being trashed even more than it would have been otherwise. At least what remained could be repaired. Without Odo's influence the Cardassians would have doubtless destroyed the station to insure that the Bajorans couldn't use it to their advantage.

Odo finds that working with the Federation, and Commander Ben Sisko, is far more to his liking than what he endured under the Cardassians. He respects Sisko, but is not reluctant to stand up to him when he feels that his authority is being challenged. In "The Passenger," when a Federation deridium shipment was due and a security officer named Primmin was sent by the Federation, Odo demanded that he remain in charge of security for the station. Sisko agreed that Odo's authority in security matters was final, and he made it clear to Primmin not to challenge or belittle Odo's authority. After all, Odo knew the station well and had even dealt with the Cardassians long before the Federation was involved with Deep Space Nine. Odo had more than authority, he possessed knowledge vital to the position of responsibility he held.

With the discovery of the stable wormhole, Odo believes that the Gamma Quadrant might well be where he's from, but he has yet to pursue that possibility as it would mean abandoning his hard earned position on the station. Although he doesn't know anything about his species, he is certain that justice is an integral part of their being because the necessity for it runs through every fiber of his body, like a racial memory. That's why he became a lawman, and when it comes to doing his job, he doesn't always follow the letter of the law. The way he figures it, laws change but justice is justice.

THE ACTOR: RENE AUBERJONOIS

Born in New York City in 1940, Rene was raised nearby in Rockland County. He took to the stage at age 16 thanks to the tutelage of noted actor, and family friend, John Houseman. The son of a news correspondent, he moved with his family to London where he continued training in the theater while he was still in high school. Rene returned to the United States to attend college, and received a Bachelor of Arts degree in Drama from Carnegie-Mellon University in Pennsylvania.

Following college he began his theatrical career in Washington, D.C. at the Arena Stage. After that he traveled between New York and Los Angeles while appearing in a number of stage productions. In San Francisco he helped found the American Conservatory Theater, and also the Mark Taper Forum in Los Angeles and the Brooklyn Academy of Music Repertory Company in New York City. The actor has starred in such stage productions as "Twelfth Night" and "Richard III."

Rene's first appearance on Broadway was with Katharine Hepburn in the musical "Coco," for which he won the prestigious Tony Award. He also received

Tony Award nominations for his performances in the Broadway productions of "The Good Doctor," "Big River," and for his role as movie mogul Buddie Fidler in the musical "City of Angels."

The actor's film debut was in the 1970 motion picture M*A*S*H. His other feature film credits include BREWSTER McCLOUD, McCABE AND MRS. MILLER, IMAGES, PETE 'N TILLIE, THE HINDENBERG (with George C. Scott), the 1976 version of KING KONG, and in POLICE ACADEMY 5. On television he appeared in such made-for-TV films as PANACHE in 1976. Rene is also a two-time Emmy Award nominee for his performance in ABC's THE LEGEND OF SLEEPY HOLLOW.

He was also the voice of Peter Parker on a Spiderman record released in the late '70s. But he also was continuing his stage work during that period as well and appeared in "King Lear" with James Earl Jones, a Joseph Papp production in the late '70s.

Auberjonois won a Best Supporting Actor in a Comedy Emmy Award for his work as Clayton Endicott III in BENSON, which starred Robert Gulliame, a series on which Rene appeared for six years. He's also known for his work on Showtime's FAERIE TALE THEATER in "The Frog Prince" with Shelley Duvall and on that program's production of "Sleeping Beauty." He's also guest starred on many television shows such as L.A. LAW, CIVIL WARS and MATLOCK. In 1993 he'll also appear in the USA Network movie WILD CARD. He is also widely known for his role as the voice of the cleaver-wielding chef in the Disney animated classic THE LITTLE MERMAID.

STAR TREK fans will recognize him as the conspiratorial assassin Colonel West in STAR TREK VI: THE UNDISCOVERED COUNTRY. (He saw part of his role edited from the film, then restored on the home video release.) This placed him on the STAR TREK scene and helped lead to him being cast in the role of Odo, Chief of Security for Deep Space Nine.

"Odo is a curmudgeon of sorts," the actor states. "He is very rigid and uptight, yet there is a wonderful humor about him. Because he does not know where he comes from or who he is, there is an existential struggle going on within him."

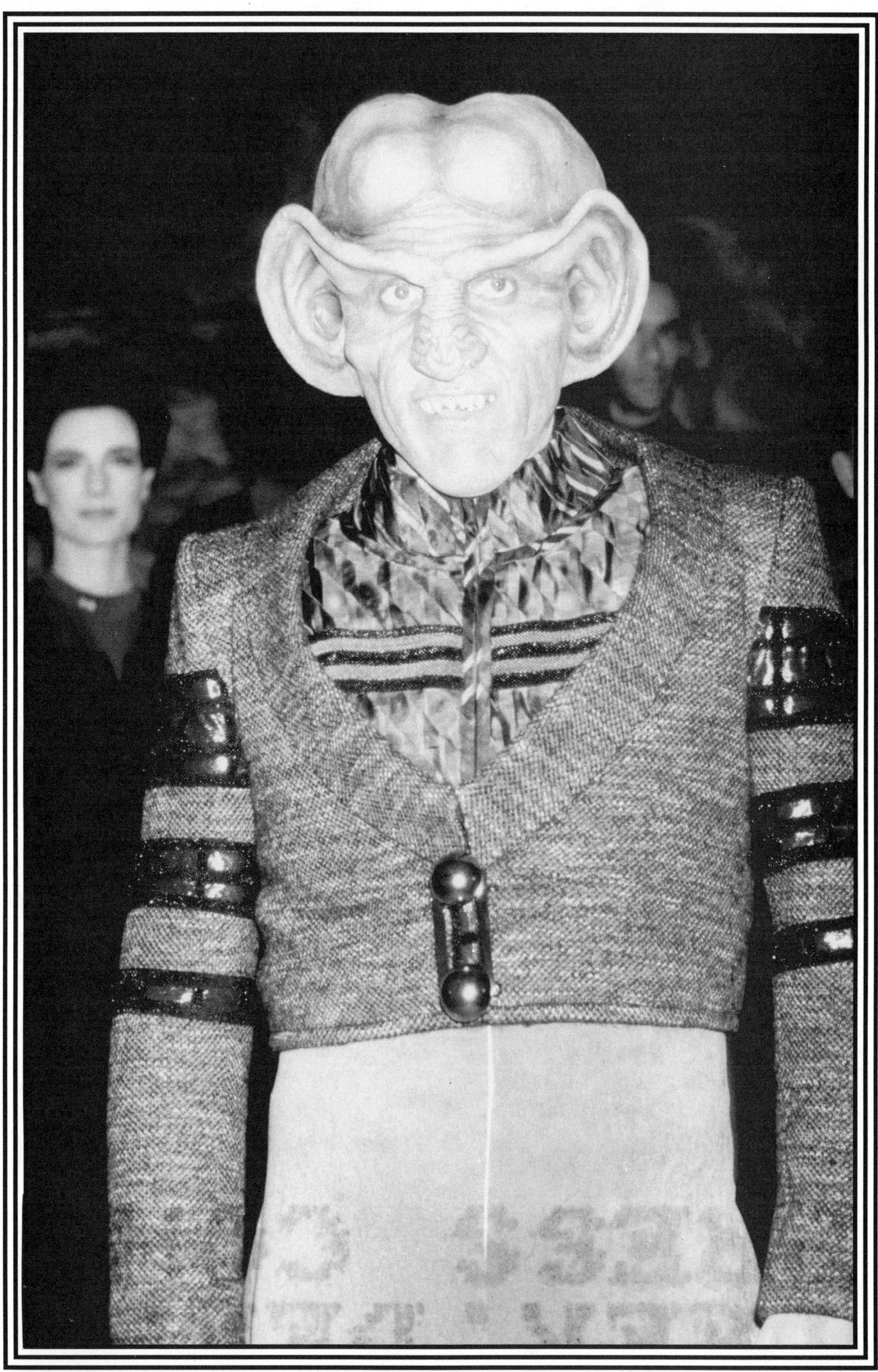

Armin Shimerman, who played the first Ferengi ever seen on THE NEXT GENERATION, revives that performance as another Ferengi, the mischievous Quark. *Photo ©1993 Ortega/Ron Galella Ltd.*

QUARK, FERENGI BARTENDER

The Ferengi race has been a part of STAR TREK: THE NEXT GENERATION since the first season of that series. They are ugly, sexist, greedy little aliens who are interested only in profit and getting their hands on anything they happen to fancy.

All of the worst things that Capitalists and businessmen have ever been accused of are considered positive traits by the Ferengi. They are taught from childhood that ethics and fairness are the province of interfering do-gooders, as represented by the people in the Federation. They also resent that they are not trusted as it makes it more difficult to cheat their clients.

Quark runs many of the entertainment concessions on Deep Space Nine including the bar/restaurant/gambling house and the holosuite brothel upstairs (where one's every fantasy can be played out). He spends most of his time behind the bar. If there is some scam being run in the sector, Quark is often involved. But beyond the malevolence, he is a charming host (in a Ferengi sort of way) and forges an interesting relationship with Sisko. They actually enjoy sparring together and now and then the Ferengi lends a hand to solve a problem for the Commander, as long as there's something in it for him.

Quark learned well in his upbringing and when he opened "Quark's Place" on the promenade of Deep Space Nine, it was with the blessings of his Cardassian hosts. They were the power controlling Bajor then and Quark knew that travelers on their way to exploit the resources of the bedeviled planet would want to stop off to slake their thirst, do a little gambling and indulge in the wide array of sexual delights available in Quark's holosuites. The Cardassians respected Quark's ruthlessness. When the Bajorans revolted and received official recognition from the Federation as a sovereign world, the Cardassians had no choice but to vacate the space station. Quark chose to remain behind, though, anticipating that this turn of events would make Deep

Space Nine busier than ever. What Quark didn't anticipate was that the only stable wormhole in the galaxy would be discovered nearby, making the space station a key stopover point for commerce involved with the otherwise distant Gamma Quadrant.

While Sisko distrusts Quark and Odo openly dislikes him, the Ferengi's influence is beyond dispute so they allow him to continue his business. While they cannot expect Quark to run a completely honest establishment (for a Ferengi that would be unheard of), it has been made clear to Quark that should he be caught cheating anyone he'll be forced to make restitution. Although an annoying prospect, this has just made Quark that much more clever.

Although a craven character at heart who is not above begging for his life, Quark is willing to deal with anyone, including a serial murderer such as was shown in the episode "The Passenger." Quark even became involved in the attempted theft of a Federation shipment by providing mercenaries for the killer, Vantaka, to use in the crime. They failed and Quark managed to escape being implicated. Quark is willing to let anyone take the rap for him. When he and a cousin cheated some aliens by selling them defective warp engines, Quark implicated his cousin who went to prison for the crime.

Quark and Odo have a history. The Security Chief was on Deep Space Nine with Quark when the Cardassians were there, so he knows what the Ferengi is capable of. Odo is more than willing to confront Quark and accuse him of whatever he believes the Ferengi to be guilty of. Presently they have a truce so Odo will not roust Quark unless he has a very good reason. In the episode "The Nagus," Odo actually saved Quark's life by uncovering the fact that the real Nagus was still alive and the Security Chief arrived just in time to prevent Quark from being assassinated when the Ferengi was locked into an airlock and threatened with being blasted into space.

Quark's effete sexist attitudes make Kira an obvious adversary. He is consumed with passion for Dax but has come on to Kira as well, once inviting her for a drink and putting his hand on her waist, whereupon she threatened him. Quark's good-natured reply was, "I love a woman in uniform!"

Quark's relationship with Commander Sisko is less certain. While Sisko tends to find Quark amusing, and for the most part harmless, he has the power to shut Quark down at any time if he chooses to.

THE ACTOR: ARMIN SHIMMERMAN

Armin was born and raised in Lakewood, New Jersey and moved to Los Angeles when he was 17. By that time, Shimmerman had decided that he would pursue a career in the legal field. But when his mother wanted to see him make more friends in Los Angeles, she got him to join a community theater which was run by one of her relatives. He landed major roles in both high school and college stage productions when he attended the University of Southern California.

After graduating from the University of California at Los Angeles, Armin moved to New York City. In New York he appeared in several regional theater productions for the Tyrone Guthrie Theater, the American Shakespeare Festival and the New York Shakespeare Festival. On Broadway, Armin appeared in such productions as "St. Joan," "I Remember Mama," and "Three Penny Opera."

Upon returning to Los Angeles, the actor made appearances on such television series as L.A. LAW, WHO'S THE BOSS, MARRIED WITH CHILDREN, ALIEN NATION ("Gimme, Gimme") and COP ROCK. Shimmerman is also widely known for his two and a half year stint in the role of Pascal on CBS's BEAUTY AND THE BEAST. He wore makeup for this character which to a small degree prepared him for what he'd encounter on THE NEXT GENERATION and DEEP SPACE NINE. On the non-STAR TREK front Shimmerman played Cousin Bernie on the critically acclaimed but low-rated series BROOKLYN BRIDGE.

Armin Shimmerman began his STAR TREK career, in successive months, portraying the "talking wedding box" that announced Deanna's engagement in the first season episode "Haven," while appearing as Letek (one of the first Ferengi seen) in "The Last Outpost." As Letek he was a more menacing character than Quark is. He appeared as a Ferengi again, this time as Bractor in "Peak Performance."

Being transformed into Quark requires three hours in the make-up chair, and it takes fifty minutes to strip it off again at the end of the shooting day. Although there is a top piece which the actor puts on his head, the face is achieved with make-up and isn't just a mask. "Michael Westmore, who is the genius behind all the make-ups on STAR TREK, doesn't believe in rubber masks," the actor explains. "He believes that they don't look real. They don't work well with the actor's face, and all of his Emmys prove that he's right." But Armin doesn't mind the three hour stint in the make-up chair. "It makes for a lot of overtime," he quips. "It's a great job! I'm making a lot of money," he says, sounding a lot like the character he portrays. The jagged Ferengi teeth are made from an alginate and just pop on over his

real teeth and are held in place by Fixodent or Poligrip. "They work!" he says enthusiastically, although it's doubtful that he'll be chosen to do an on-air product endorsement by the manufacturer.

Armin's make-up lady who does the rigorous and meticulous job of applying his Ferengi make-up is Karen Westerfield. She was part of the team which won an Emmy for the make-up on THE NEXT GENERATION in 1992. The look of the Ferengi was originally designed by Michael Westmore and Shimmerman created much of the individual Ferengi characterization when he played the first Ferengi ever seen in the STAR TREK universe. In describing what having the make-up applied is like, it starts with the head piece. "It's delicately applied around the eyes. Then the mask [facial make-up] has to be joined to the ears on the helmet. The scarlet around the eyes is what I love the most because the eyes immediately pop out because of the scarlet." The costume was designed by Robert Blackman. "After about the second hour I begin to transform psychologically and mentally into Quark and I become an extrovert."

Shimmerman has started making appearances at STAR TREK conventions and he describes them as being, "Like news conferences. You go out and you take questions and you try to answer as best you can and sometimes you make things up.

Shimmerman describes the Ferengi as being, "A group of aliens who are the capitalists of the universe. We're out to make a buck and accumulate as much money as we can. I think of ourselves as the robber barons like the Carnegies, Rockerfellers and people like that." When asked whether Quark prefers money or women, Armin replies, "That's a tough decision."

In describing the concessions he has at Quark's place, he says, "I have my own ATM machines. I run the bar. I run something called the holosuites upstairs from my bar. Whatever fantasies you have, I can find a program so that you'll be satisfied upstairs in the holosuites, and I make a little profit off of that." Shimmerman also says that the ears of the Ferengi are their erogenous zones.

When asked why no women Ferengis have ever been seen on any of the STAR TREK series, Armin explains that the reason is that, "Ferengi females are all nude." This is not just a glib throwaway line as in "The Last Outpost," when Letek sees Tasha Yar, he remarks how disgusting it is that the humans make their women wear clothes.

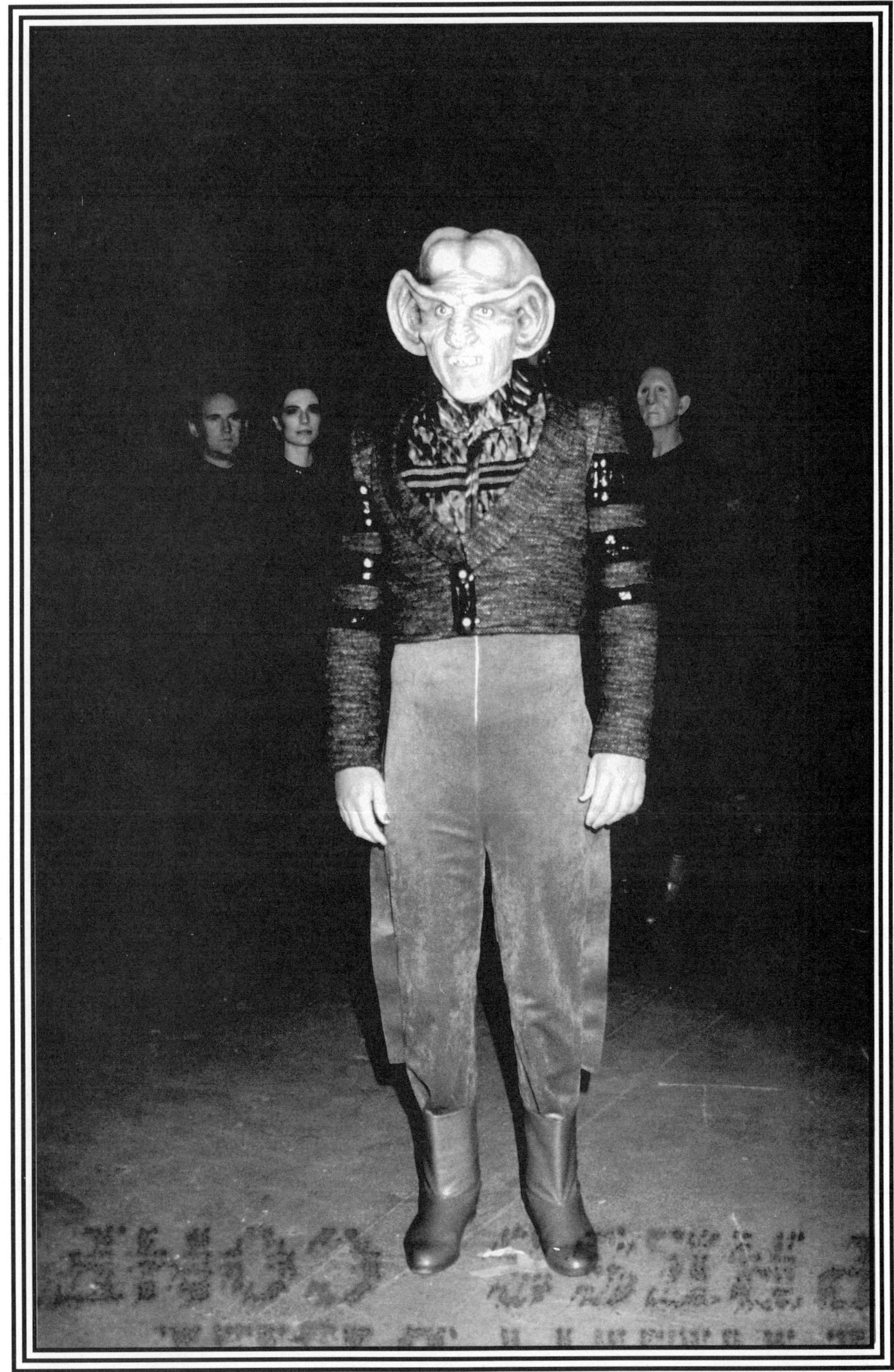

As the Ferengi Quark, actor Armin Shimerman doesn't mind the three hours it takes to put on his make-up because he gets paid overtime! ***Photo ©1993 Ortega/Ron Galella Ltd.***

Avery Brooks answers questions from the press when the full cast of DEEP SPACE NINE greets the public for the first time.

Photo ©1993 Ortega/Ron Galella Ltd.

COMMANDER BENJAMIN SISKO

by Alex Burleson

Sisko met his future wife, Jennifer, at Gilgo Beach in California. This was soon after graduating from Starfleet Academy and before he received his first posting as a young ensign on a starship. They married and after five years produced a son they named Jake.

They took Jake along with them when Sisko was promoted to full Commander and assigned as First Officer aboard the USS Saratoga. The starship was transporting civilians when admiral Hanson ordered the ship diverted to Wolf 359 to intercept the Borg. At that engagement the Borg were led by a kidnapped Jean-Luc Picard who had been turned into "Locutus," spokesborg in the race's dealings with humans.

The Saratoga's Vulcan Captain, Storil, was killed in the initial attack and Sisko was forced into command. He found all of the bridge officers (Garcia, Delaney, Tomamoto and Storil) dead, with the exception of Second Officer Lt. Hranok, a Bolian. They managed to evacuate the survivors, but Sisko was shattered by the death of his wife. She was killed during the engagement with the Borg. Benjamin was separated from Jake on the ship but reunited with his son in the escape pod, which launched seconds before the Borg destroyed the ship. Sisko had been forced away from his wife's body by the strength of the Bolian, and later had to face the fact that he never truly left.

He was assigned to the Mars Utopia Planetia Shipyards (where the Enterprise-D was constructed). Three years after Wolf 359, Sisko was ordered to take command of an abandoned Cardassian space station in orbit of the planet Bajor, which had recently overthrown the multidecade occupation of their homeland. Sisko was prepared to reject the order and quit Starfleet altogether. He'd requested an Earth assignment because he's a single father with a son to raise. He decided to give Bajor a try which proved key to overcoming his grief. He is a man who carried with him the guilt and anguish of the death of his wife. Until he had an emotional passage in the premiere episode, as he confronted aliens in the guise of people from his past, he could not move on with his life. His important work on Deep Space Nine gives him a new direction, but his is still very much a life framed by tragedy.

Had Sisko not been able to expunge the guilt, he may have ended up like another Benjamin. Benjamin Maxwell was taken into custody by the Enterprise after he killed hundreds of Cardassians, in an attempt to extract revenge for the death of his wife and children at the hands of the Cardassians. (Deep Space Nine's Chief of Operations, Miles O'Brien, was Tactical Officer to Capt. Maxwell on the USS Rutledge before being transferred to the Enterprise.)

Sisko had a very tense meeting with Captain Jean-Luc Picard when the Enterprise arrived at Bajor. (Picard: "Have we met before?" Sisko: "Yes, we met in battle.") Sisko was still unable to separate Picard from Locutus. He later realized that Picard was victimized by the Borg when he was kidnapped and that his anger was misplaced. He learned that lesson after an unplanned stop in the middle of a wormhole. Ben and Lt. Jadzia Dax (who was once Ben's elderly male mentor, Curzon Dax, before the Curzon host body of the Trill died) traveled into the wormhole and became the first known visitors to the Gamma Quadrant. (It is later discovered than an archaeologist named Vash preceded them, with help from the "Q" entity.)

Sisko negotiated with the aliens who live in the wormhole and his own tragic story proved instrumental in teaching crucial facets of humanity to the aliens who have to struggle to understand how linear time operates. They also allowed him to finally release the grief he had stored up inside. The catharsis is most apparent in his next meeting with Picard, in which he withdraws his request for a transfer.

Commander Sisko was happy to see O'Brien's wife, Keiko, open a school on DS9 and has learned to balance the needs of a civilian population with a Starfleet facility. He has found peace of mind on Bajor, and seeing Jennifer again allowed "her" to help him learn to accept the loss. When he communicates with the aliens once more they will presumably again take the forms of his own memories.

THE ACTOR: AVERY BROOKS

Born and raised in Indiana, Avery Brooks attended Oberlin College, Indiana University and later Rutgers University where he was the first black MFA graduate in the fields of acting and directing.

Brooks spent more than ten years in the theater performing the title role in the biographical play "Paul Robeson," written by Phillip Hayes Dean. He performed the role on Broadway, at the Westwood Playhouse in Los Angeles and at the Kennedy Center in Washington, D.C.. He also played Paul Robeson in the play "Are You Now Or Have You Ever Been?" in 1978 both on and off Broadway.

His stage credits include the lead in Shakespeare's "Othello" which he performed at Washington, D.C.'s Folger Shakespeare Theatre. Brooks also appeared in Ntozake Shange's "A Photograph" and "Spell #7" for the New York Shakespeare Festival. His musical abilities and powerful voice landed him the role of Malcolm X in the American Music Theatre Festival production of the Anthony Davis opera "X: The Life And Times of Malcolm X." Avery Brooks has also performed with such jazz artists as Butch Morris, Henry Threadgill, Jon Hendricks, Joseph Jarman and Lester Bowie. Brooks was also the host of THE MUSICAL LEGACY OF ROLAND HAYES, an award-winning documentary.

Avery Brooks is perhaps best known to the public at large for his portrayal of Hawk in the ABC series SPENCER FOR HIRE. The performer has also done extensive work with the Smithsonian's program in Black American culture. On the PBS American Playhouse he had the title role in the film SOLOMON NORTHUP'S ODYSSEY. Brooks played Uncle Tom in the Showtime production of UNCLE TOM'S CABIN for which he received a CableACE Award nomination.

Avery Brooks was actually one of the last members of the main DS9 crew to be cast. Speculation was rife regarding who would ultimately portray Commander Benjamin Sisko, the crucial, leading role on the show. MacGYVER's Harry Dean Anderson was rumored to be in the running at one point. The racial background of the character was not determined until Brooks was cast in the part. Tryouts for the role of Sisko involved actors of varied backgrounds, from both Europe and the United States, including Siddig El Fadil, who would be cast for DEEP SPACE NINE in a different role. At one point, serious thought was given to the idea of making the Commander a woman, a concept that was ultimately watered down to having a woman as Sisko's second in command.

Avery Brooks differs from previous Star Trek leading men in that he had already been part of a high-profile television series before his involvement in DEEP

SPACE NINE. The roles of Hawk and Sisko are world apart. Brooks retains his hair for his role on DEEP SPACE NINE, and Sisko is, without a doubt, a much nicer guy than the bald-pated Hawk.

Brooks won the role of Ben Sisko in a field of hundreds of applicants, of all racial groups (even aliens were considered for the role). Rick Berman confirmed that Tony Todd auditioned for the role of Sisko. Todd played the title role in the horror film CANDYMAN, was Worf's brother Commander Kurn in THE NEXT GENERATION's third season "Sins of the Father" and in "Redemption." Carl Weathers and James Earl Jones were also considered, as was the young actor who wound up as the new Chief Medical Officer of Deep Space Nine.

Outside of television, Brooks has been associated with Rutgers University for 20 years and also taught at Oberlin College and Case Western Reserve University. Avery Brooks is also a tenured professor of theater at the Mason Gross School of the Arts.

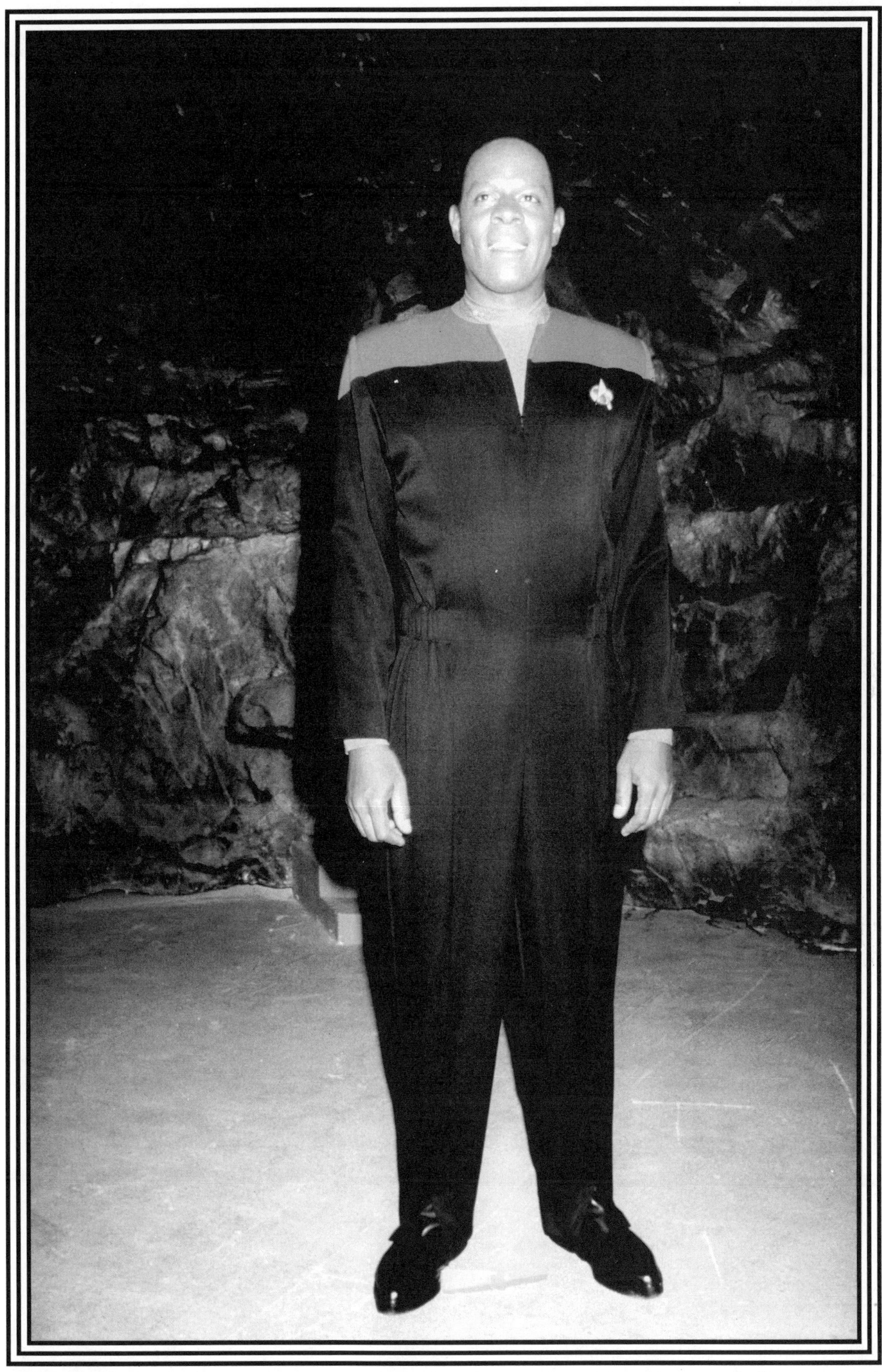

On DEEP SPACE NINE, Avery Brooks plays Commander Ben Sisko, the Federation officer put in charge of overseeing the Bajoran space station known as Deep Space Nine. ***Photo ©1993 Ortega/Ron Galella Ltd.***

KEIKO O'BRIEN

The wife of Miles O'Brien, she has a three year old daughter by Miles, whom she met and married while both were still stationed on the Enterprise. When Miles was offered the assignment of Chief of Operations on Deep Space Nine, it was not welcome news for Keiko. On the station Keiko has found that her expertise as a botanist is not much in demand, and initially she was angry and frustrated because she did not feel as though she was doing anything useful. What had been a good career move for him had put Keiko's career on hold, seemingly indefinitely. But finally she found a useful place for herself by opening a school for the children who live on the station.

Although Keiko has been a semi-regular on THE NEXT GENERATION and now is on DEEP SPACE NINE, the experiences of her character have largely been mundane. In the episode "Disaster," the pregnant Keiko gave birth in Ten Forward without a doctor to assist and Worf acting as midwife using what he learned from a computer simulation. When her husband was taken over by a threatening alien entity, it was all she could do to protect her baby. The character did no real interacting with the transformed Miles O'Brien other than to cower. For a semi-regular, Keiko has been very underused and barely has a recognizable personality. Thus far on DEEP SPACE NINE this situation has not improved, and in fact she has not appeared in several episodes, ostensibly because her character is away on Earth visiting her aged mother.

THE ACTOR: ROSALIND CHAO

Rosalind Chao appeared on BEAUTY AND THE BEAST and has been seen in several films and mini-series. Her NEXT GENERATION appearances include "Data's Day," "The Wounded," "Disaster," "Power Play," "In Theory," "Rascals," "Night Terrors," etc. She is a semi-regular on DEEP SPACE NINE.

JAKE SISKO

Jake is an army brat who doesn't remember life on Earth. The fourteen year old boy has been aboard four different starships and stationed on two different planets before arriving on Deep Space Nine with his father. The transient lifestyle has taught him how to scope out a new terrain, and assimilate into it quickly. At the same time he has an inner fear of forming intimate friendships because he loses them so quickly. He has found a kindred spirit in an unlikely place—Quark's nephew, Nog. He's become close friends with the Ferengi boy, and when Nog was barred from attending the Federation school by his father, Rom, Jake took upon it himself to secretly tutor Nog, who may well grow up into a very different kind of Ferengi.

Jake dreams of going to live on Earth. He collects holodeck programs of various Earth locales which he uses to try to fulfill his fantasy. Deep inside he knows that his mother would still be alive if they had not been living in space. His father promised that there would be other kids on the station, although it turned out that there are only a few. But Nog, regarded by Jake's father and others as a bad influence, has more sides to him than the adults normally see.

Jake is very close to his dad and they're buddies to such a degree that the Commander is plagued with feelings that he's not doing the job of parenting very well, and that maybe more discipline is required. But as with many adolescents, Ben is discovering that his son is growing up faster than he realized, particularly when he discovers that Jake and Nog like to watch girls arriving on the station.

THE ACTOR: CIRROC LOFTON

Cirroc was born in Los Angeles. He entered acting at the age of 9 when he appeared in an educational program entitled "Agency for Instructional Technology." In describing his acting debut, Cirroc says, "I have always loved to act, in fact I starred in our elementary school plays—I even portrayed Martin Luther King, Jr."

Cirroc has appeared in a number of commercials for McDonalds, Tropicana Orange Juice and Kellogg's Rice Krispies. He made his feature debut in 1992 in the Universal comedy movie BEETHOVEN, which was a surprise hit. It has not been announced whether he will appear in the sequel to BEETHOVEN.

Lofton enjoys basketball and bike riding. He is continuing his schooling while working on DEEP SPACE NINE and hopes to some day become a doctor. Cirroc compares himself to his character Jake Sisko. "Jake is very close to his father and they are just like buddies. My father and I are buddies, too." Cirroc lives in Los Angeles with his mother and sister.

A tense-looking Cirroc Lofton at the grand presentation for DEEP SPACE NINE held September 2, 1992. In the background are Terry Ferrell, Siddig El Fadil, and Rene Auberjonois. *Photo ©1993 Ortega/Ron Galella Ltd.*

Rene Auberjonois, who plays security chief Odo on DEEP SPACE NINE.

TALES FROM DEEP SPACE: EPISODE GUIDE

CREDITS

Teleplay by Michael Piller
Story by Rick Berman
and Michael Piller

Directed by David Carson

Regular Cast:
Avery Brooks as Commander Benjamin Sisko
Rene Auberjonois as Odo
Siddig El Fadil as Doctor Bashir
Terry Farrell as Lieutenant Dax
Cirroc Lofton as Jake Sisko
Colm Meaney as Chief O'Brien
Armin Shimerman as Quark
Nana Visitor as Major Kira

Guest Stars:
Patrick Stewart as Jean-Luc Picard
Camille Saviola
Felecia M. Bell
Marc Alaimo
Joel Swetow: Gul Jasal
Aron Eisenerg: Nog
Stephen Davies: Tactical Officer
Max Grodenchik: Ferengi Pit Boss
Steve Rankin: Cardassian Officer
Lily Mariye: Ops Officer
Cassandra Byram: Communications Officer
John Noah Hertzler: Vulcan Captain
April Grace: Transporter Chief
Kevin McDermott: Alien Batter
Parker Whitman: Cardassian Officer
William Powell-Blair: Cardassian Officer
Frank Owen Smith: Curzon
Lynnda Fergusson: Doran
Megan Butler: Lieutenant
Stephen Power: Chanting Monk
Thomas Hobson: Young Jake
Donald Hotton: Monk #1
Gene Armor: Bajoran Bureaucrat
Diana Cignoni: Dabo Girl
Judi Durand: Computer Voice
Majel Barrett: Computer Voice

Additional credits:
Music and Series Main Title Theme: Dennis McCarthy
Director of Photography: Marvin Rush
Editing: Robert Lederman
Production design: Herman Zimmerman
Producer: Peter Lauritson
Supervising Producer: David Livingston
Executive Producers: Rick Berman and Michael Piller
Associate Producer: Steve Oster
Casting by Junie Lowry-Johnson, C.S.A., and Ron Surma
Unit Production Manager: Robert della Santina
First Assistant Director: Venita Ozols-Graham
Second Assistant Director: Alisa Matlovsky
Second Second Assistant Director: Michael Baxter
Costume Designer: Robert Blackman
Visual Effects Supervisor: Robert Legato
Make-up Design and Supervision: Michael Westmore
Senior Art Supervisor/Technical Consultant: Michael Okuda
Senior Illustrator/ Technical Consultant: Rick Sternbach
Additional Visual Effects Supervision: Gary Hutzel
Post Production Supervisor: Terri Martinez
Art Director: Randy McIlvain
Set Decorator: Mickey S. Michaels
Set Design: Joseph Hodges/ Alan S. Kaye/ Nathan Crowley
Script Supervisor: Judi Brown
Special Effects: Gary Monak
Property Master: Joe Longo
Chief Lighting Technician: William Peets
First Company Grip: Bob Sorda
Wardrobe Supervisor: Carol Kunz
Hair Designer: Candy Neal
Make-up Artists: Janna Phillips/ Craig Reardon/ Jill Rockow
Hair Stylists: Richard Sabre/ Gerald Solomon
Sound Mixer: Bill Gocke
Camera Operator: Joe Chess, S.O.C.
Key Costumers:
Maurice Palinski
Phyllis Corcoran-Woods
Jerry Bono
Patty Borggese-Taylor
Visual Effects Coordinators:
Michael Backauskas
Cari Thomas
Judy Elkins
Mari Hotaki

Visual Effects Associate: Laura Lang

Scenic Artists: Doug Drexler and Denise Okuda
Illustrator: Ricardo F. Delgado
Video Playback Operator: Joe ?
Video Consultant: Liz Radley
Music Editor: Stephen M. Rowe
Supervising Sound Editor: Bill Wistrom
Supervising Sound Effects Editor: Jim Wolvington
Re-Recording Mixers:
Chris Haire, C.A.S.
Doug Davey
Richard Morrison, C.A.S.
Production Coordinator: Heidi Julian
Post-Production Coordinator: Dawn Hernandez
Assistant Editor: Eugene Wood
Visual Effects Assistant Editor: Ed Hoffmeister
Pre-Production Associate: Lolita Fatjo
Production Associate: Kim Fitzgerald
Stunt Coordinator: Dennis Madalone
Construction Coordinator: Richard J. Bayard
Transportation Coordinator: Stewart Satterfield
Science Consultant: Naren Shankar
Casting Executive: Helen Mossler, C.S.A.
Motion Control Photography by IMAGE "G"
Video Optical Effects by DIGITAL MAGIC
Special Video Compositing: CIS Hollywood
Editing Facilities: Unitel Video
Post Production Sound by Modern Sound
Main Title Design: Dan Curry
Matte Painting: Illusion Arts
Miniatures:
Brazil Fabrication and Design
Gregory Jein, Inc.
Computer Animation:
Rhythm & Hues, Inc.
Vision Art Design & Animation

"EMISSARY"

TEASER: BATTLE WITH THE BORG

The two-part pilot begins with a black screen. A brief text is run, explaining the background of Jean-Luc Picard's capture by the Borg ("The Best of Both Worlds, Parts One and Two") and his role in the battle of Wolf 359, followed by the first image in the pilot: Picard/Locutus on a viewscreen, demanding the complete surrender of Federation forces. The view shifts to a close-up of Lieutenant Commander Benjamin Sisko reacting to the Borg ultimatum on the battle bridge of the USS Saratoga.

The view moves back, revealing the ship's command team at work: a blue-skinned Bolan Lieutenant as Tactical Officer, human ensigns at Ops and Con positions, and the ship's Captain, a Vulcan, who puts the ship on Red Alert.

The view in space reveals various Federation ships circling the Borg cube. One ship (identified as the USS Melbourne in the first draft of the script) fires its phasers at the cube in a suicide run, only to have half of its saucer vaporized by the deadly Borg weaponry. Then the Borg beams lock on to the Saratoga, draining its shields slowly away, and a huge explosion rocks the bridge. When the smoke clears, Sisko staggers to his feet. A woman ensign lies dead on the floor with a huge wound, and the rest of the battle bridge crew, except Sisko and the Bolan officer, are dead.

Sisko calls for damage reports. Vast damage is everywhere, including a warp core failure mere minutes away. Assessing the situation, Sisko calls for immediate evacuation of the vessel. The situation is obviously hopeless. With a general evacuation underway and the ship utterly defenseless, a dazed Sisko seeks his wife and son in their quarters, which are a twisted mass of smoke-filled wreckage. He first finds his son Jake, a nine-year-old boy who is unconscious but alive. Nearby lies Jennifer Sisko, her beautiful face oddly calm in death; the lower half of her is pinned beneath weighty debris. Desperately, he claws at the rubble, but to no avail; the Bolan tactical officer must drag him away from his efforts and off to the escape pods. In shock, Sisko sits staring out the window of the pod as it breaks away from the doomed starship. The receding Saratoga can be seen reflected in the window before Sisko's face. A quick field reversal shows the ship explode in a blinding flash; returning to the shot of Sisko in the window, we see the Commander's face illuminated by the glare of the explosion.

The scene fades out, revealing a title establishing a new timeframe: Stardate 46379.1: Three Years Later. Jake Sisko, now twelve, is sitting fishing by a river with an old-fashioned fishing pole. Into this idyllic scene steps Commander Sisko, in full uniform, who has come to get Jake for their imminent departure for Bajor. Unsure about their new assignment, the boy turns to his father for assurance, but it is obvious that the elder Sisko is covering his own uncertainties for the boy's sake. A voice from the bridge reveals that they have already reached Bajor; the riverside is just a computer simulation. Sisko ends the program, revealing the familiar black-and-yellow grid of a Federation holodeck. The two Siskos leave the holodeck and pause at an observation window to look out at their new home: the space station Deep Space Nine.

OPENING CREDIT SEQUENCE

After the teaser, "Emissary" proceeds with the first look at the opening titles for DEEP SPACE NINE. A starfield, partially obscured by a nebula fills the screen, as an asteroid trailing a vaporous trail drifts into sight from the left. As the asteroid passes, the camera turns and follows it briefly, as if the viewer were drifting along right behind it, the vapor trail streaking by. Then the viewer's perspective shifts, leaving the celestial body to drift away. The viewer drifts to the right, and a plain starfield fills the screen until a space station can be seen in the lower right-hand corner of the screen. The title STAR TREK: DEEP SPACE NINE appears above it, filling the middle third of the screen.

As this image is held, a small ship disembarks from the space station and draws ever closer, turning its underside to the viewer as it, in turn, fills the screen with the blue light of its propulsion units and disappears by way of the upper left side of the screen. For a moment the blue glare of its exhaust obscures all other images, only to fade and reveal a close-up shot of the space station, now filling the screen.

The credits begin with a nod to Gene Roddenberry as the creator of STAR TREK. The principal cast are all featured in turn as a series of slow dissolves reveal different views of the station, each shot slowly drifting by at a languid pace. First, a view from beneath reveals that the station consists of three rings, the centermost glowing redly with the emissions from the power array. Another fade reveals a view of the outermost ring from the outside, only to be replaced by a view from inside the rings, centering on one of the three linking spokes of the station and the arching docking ring that rises from it. Another fade takes in a view of the central Ops tower from above, light emerging from its many windows. The last shot of the opening sequence lingers upon an outer view of the third rings from a slightly more distant perspective, revealing much of the station, motionless against a starfield, as a small ship slowly approaches to dock.

One visual element is missing in this final shot, as it represents a story element which would only be introduced in the course of the plot of "Emissary." This, of course, is the wormhole. An effects shot of it appearing against the starfield would be added to this sequence for the regular episodes of DEEP SPACE NINE.

The entire effect of this sequence— designed by Robert Delgado and realized by Dan Curry and his special effects team— is radically different from that of THE NEXT GENERATION. While that show's opening upholds the classic STAR TREK motif of frenetic movement through space, the opening to DEEP SPACE NINE is extremely calm and restful by comparison. The mysteries of space unfold themselves slowly before our eyes, and the station moves into view as if discovered quite by chance.

FIRST ACT:
SISKO TAKES CHARGE

A medium shot of Deep Space Nine reveals the Enterprise is docked there as Commander Sisko, in his first Station Log entry, reveals that the Starfleet flagship has already been at DS9 for two days. It delivered much of Sisko's staff, including Chief Miles O'Brien, who has transferred to this new command as Sisko's Chief Operations Officer. Now that the Cardassians have finally abandoned Bajor, Starfleet has agreed to move in and take over operations of the space station. Now Bajor hopes to join the Federation. But the Bajoran provisional government is a precarious setup at best, making Sisko's new assignment an unwanted challenge.

The first glimpse of the station's interior is of Sisko's face behind a door. The door is basically a large disc with gear cogs which opens, somewhat laboriously, only after a clearly impatient Sisko has been waiting for some time. (Part of this scene, trimmed from the final version but present in Michael Piller's first-draft script, actually has Chief O'Brien open the door manually.) Sisko, Jake and O'Brien walk through the door into the promenade, which is in complete shambles. The noise of hammers clanging and the flash of flickering lights fill the cloudy atmosphere; it is unclear whether these are the sounds of repairs being made or of more destruction. O'Brien, filling Sisko in on things, reveals that the departing Cardassians "celebrated" their departure by stripping the station of everything of value; some Bajoran shopkeepers were even killed in the looting. O'Brien and Major Kira, the Bajoran attaché, have put all hands to work on primary systems, leaving the Promenade largely unattended except by a few shopkeepers who are salvaging what they can, including a surly Ferengi barman who glances up from packing his wares to watch the three humans go by.

Suddenly, a Bajoran monk emerges from the ruins of a temple and invites Sisko inside. But Sisko must go see Major Kira, and says that he will come another time. The monk echoes Sisko's words with hidden meaning, and watches as the Commander goes on his way.

First, O'Brien escorts the Siskos to their quarters. To Jake, the set up is distressingly spartan. As before, Sisko tries to cover his own feelings but the boy obviously sees through this. With this matter clearly unresolved, Sisko follows O'Brien to Ops, where he discovers that the office is located high above all other stations, in order to assure a clear view of everything— a typical Cardassian touch.

Kira and Sisko get off to a contentious start, thanks largely to the Major's abrasive personality, but Sisko makes a plea for cooperation which seems to register somewhat. Their conversation is abruptly interrupted by a break-in on the Promenade, and Sisko follows Kira to investigate.

A young Ferengi, Nog, and an unidentified larger alien are seen stealing some ore samples, only to have their escape blocked by Security Chief Odo. Trapped, the larger alien takes a deadly bladed weapon from his belt and hurls it at Odo. The Security Chief does not flinch as the weapon flies straight toward the center of his head. Instead, Odo's head becomes an amorphous, plasmoid mass which the weapon passes directly through. His head then reforms and he attacks the alien thief, only to have their struggle interrupted by a phaser blast from Sisko.

Odo's irritation at this interruption is cut short by the arrival of Quark, the Ferengi barkeeper seen earlier. Quark knows better than to try to negotiate with Odo so he turns to the new boss in town, Sisko, and tries to get him to set Nog (his nephew) free. Sisko will not release the Ferengi boy. Later, Major Kira observes that the greedy Quark was probably behind the theft anyway. Sisko replies that he plans to use the boy to bargain with Quark. This puzzles Major Kira. Before he can explain it to her, O'Brien reminds Sisko that Captain Picard wants to speak with him on board the Enterprise. Sisko is obviously not looking forward this.

**SECOND ACT:
THE REVELATION OF THE ORB**

Picard, seated in his conference room on board the Enterprise (with DS9 visible out the window), greets Commander Sisko as he enters. Picard is friendly, unaware of Sisko's feelings about their previous encounter until Sisko mentions that they had met before. This catches Picard off guard, as he has no recollection of ever meeting Sisko. Sisko explains that they met at the battle of Wolf 359. Suddenly aware that Sisko's view of him is something determined by a twist of fate that Picard had no choice in, he withdraws, as Sisko already has, to a curt, chilly mode of communication that is all protocol.

Sisko and Picard discuss the Bajoran situation in the wake of the Cardassian withdrawal. Although Bajoran freedom fighters/terrorists (take your pick, depending on your perspective) have taken credit for the end of the occupation, it remains likely that the Cardassians may have left simply because they had stripped the planet of Bajor of all its resources. Finding it no longer profitable, they were quick to leave it to its original inhabitants.

Sisko is not particularly keen on discussing the situation at any length with Picard. Picard notes that Sisko has already objected to the assignment. Sisko counters by expressing an interest in returning to civilian service. Picard, by now quite distant in his tone, tells Sisko that he'll start looking for a replacement right away, but that Sisko must still fulfill his duties until then. On that note, Sisko breaches protocol by rising and coldly thanking Captain Picard for the briefing.

Sisko returns to Deep Space Nine, where he soon becomes embroiled in a discussion with Quark regarding the fate of his nephew Nog; a bemused Odo looks on.

Sisko is willing to cut a deal with the wily Ferengi, a plea bargain of sorts, but only if Quark and his people will stay on the station and keep the Promenade going. This, Sisko wagers, will inspire others to stay and keep life going as close to normal as is possible for DS9. Quark really has no choice; if he does not agree, Nog will be spending his formative years in prison on Bajor.

Odo, at first bewildered by Sisko's desire for Quark to become, in Sisko's words, "a community leader," finds the upshot of this conflict rather amusing. This may actually be the first time Odo has ever seen anyone out-Ferengi the Ferengi, and he likes it.

Leaving the scene of his first success on DS9, Sisko makes his way down to the still-ruined Promenade, where he discovers Major Kira moving debris. (In the first-draft script, she is using a shovel; in the pilot as filmed she and Sisko use their hands— perhaps because no design for a Bajoran shovel had been devised.) She is channelling her anger at the apathy of those Bajorans who have abandoned the station through this seemingly futile work. She's surprised when her sarcastic comment about Starfleet officers never getting their hands dirty prompts Sisko to join her in her efforts.

As they work side by side, they discuss the problems of the Bajoran provisional government. A shaky structure, it seems doomed to fall quite soon unless the spiritual leader of Bajor, Kai Opaka, calls for unity. Unfortunately no one, not even Kira, has been able to contact the Kai. But suddenly, the Bajoran monk previously encountered during Sisko's first tour of the Promenade appears again, telling Sisko that it is time for Sisko to meet Kai Opaka.

Sisko goes to the planet surface. We see the ruins of Bajor's ancient capitol, with many exotic buildings, vaguely reminiscent of Ottoman minarets, still standing, and an imposing monastery dominating the largest hill overlooking the city. It is here that Sisko meets Kai Opaka, a short, middle-aged woman in robes and a headpiece whose right ear bears a far more elaborate array of ritual earrings than is seen on the average Bajoran. She speaks obscurely of Sisko's arrival, which he takes to mean as an appreciation of the Federation's new presence in the area, but which really refers to the arrival of Sisko as an individual. He is somewhat perturbed to find himself regarded as some sort of Messianic figure. He has come to discuss pragmatic political realities but is instead being drawn into a dubious metaphysical discussion. His discomfort increases as Kai Opaka begins talking of pagh, a Bajoran spiritual concept, and starts to touch his earlobe. Eventually, she seems satisfied that Sisko is the one expected by prophecy, whatever his own misgivings might be, and leads the Commander down a spiral stairway that appears in a place occupied by a shallow pool.

Deep below the monastery, in a shadowy, candle-lit chamber, Kai Opaka shows Sisko an ark which when opened, reveals a glowing green Orb within. Suddenly, its verdant illumination spins out and overwhelms Sisko. He suddenly finds himself on a beach, in bathing clothes, carrying a tray of drinks. The hot sand begins to burn his bare feet before he can even begin to think, and he rushes for the first refuge he can find. It happens to be a beach blanket occupied by a beautiful woman. This leads to an embarrassing collision. The confusion is heightened when he realizes that she is his wife Jennifer, and that he is somehow reliving their first meeting.

At first this re-run seems likely to be a disaster, but, regaining his composure, Sisko summons enough charm to keep Jennifer's attention. He is actually beginning to enjoy this strange experience when he sees the Orb floating above the beach, visible only to him. Suddenly he is back in the underground chamber, and Kai Opaka is there, closing the ark and explaining the Orb to him.

The Orb, she reveals, was found in the skies ten thousand years earlier(as opposed to the mere thousand years in the original draft of the pilot), the first of nine over the millennia, believed to originate in the Celestial Temple. Desirous of their power, the Cardassians have stolen all but the first Orb, which has been safely secured beneath the monastery for countless ages. So far, the Cardassians have not been able to learn the secret of these seemingly mystical artifacts. Kai Opaka fears that this would bring about a spiritual disaster. It seems that.it is up to the reluctant Sisko, still shaken by his temporal displacement experience, to locate the Celestial Temple and warn the unseen prophets of the imminent danger. To this end, Kai Opaka gives the Orb to Sisko, in order that he might learn something from it. This quest, she tells him, is as much for his own spiritual benefit (his own pagh) as it is for the people of Bajor.

THIRD ACT: BASHIR AND DAX ARRIVE

Sisko returns to Deep Space Nine and looks in on his son Jake, who is sleeping. It seems as if it has been a terribly long time since he last set eyes on the boy. But this reunion is interrupted when Major Kira calls Sisko to the Promenade.

It seems that Sisko's blackmail ploy has worked. Quark has re-opened his bar, which also serves as a casino, and people are arriving en masse, eager for some diversion and obviously having a good time. While discussing the faults of Bajoran ale, "Don't trust an ale from a god fearing people," is the Ferengi's advice, Quark makes an offhand comment regarding his nephew's situation, slyly reminding Sisko of his end of the deal without explicitly asking the Commander to release the boy. Quark knows a verbal contract when he's party to one, especially a dubious one such as this. He knows that the Commander must now fulfill his side of the bargain.

Later, Sisko goes to greet two new arrivals, key members of his basic staff. One of these is the young and cocky Doctor Julian Bashir (named Julian Amoros in the first draft script), who obviously has a hankering for the beautiful Lieutenant Jadzia Dax, the new science officer. Dax appears to be in her twenties, but she is also over three hundred years old. Dax is a Trill, the symbiotic race first encountered in the NEXT GENERATION episode "The Host." Inside the young humanoid body resides an ancient slug-like being; the two minds merged to create a gestalt personality.

Dax's previous incarnation was in the host body of Curzon, who was a close friend of young Benjamin Sisko. They are still friends, but this is the first time that Sisko has met his old friend in this new body, a transition that clearly takes some getting used to.

This poses no problem for Doctor Bashir, whose knowledge of the slug inside Dax in no way detracts from his rather callow interest in the external beauty of her body. Dax herself seems quite bemused by his interest, but the Trill cannot view these matters in the same fashion as humans.

While Sisko and Dax go off to renew their acquaintance, Major Kira escorts Doctor Bashir to what is left of the medical facility. Bashir, oddly enough, seems excited by the primitiveness of the situation, referring with some glee to his interest in "frontier medicine." Kira is offended by this, pointing out that Bashir's "frontier" is her home, and that the Bajorans are facing real medical emergencies of great proportions. (In the original draft of the script the best she can manage is a quip about the adventure of controlling the dysentery on DS9. The line as shot is better. It focuses on a more dramatic problem.

Meanwhile, Sisko has given Dax the Orb to study. Dax has the computer interface with Bajoran databanks and sets about to find out what portions of space were the source of the Orbs. Suddenly, the Orb does to her what it did to Sisko; she finds herself in an operating room, reliving the transfer of the Trill to her body from that of the dying Curzon. And just as suddenly she is back in her new laboratory, shaken by the experience.

O'Brien prepares to take his final leave of the Enterprise. (A scene in the original draft of the script has him confronting Keiko in their quarters; she is extremely unhappy about the move. But in fact, with this scene cut, Keiko does not appear in the pilot at all.) Heading down to his favorite Transporter Room, he tries to beam away without any farewells, but Captain Picard catches up with him and mans the controls himself, giving O'Brien a proper sendoff.

FOURTH ACT:
RETURN OF THE CARDASSIANS

Later, back on Deep Space Nine, O'Brien informs Sisko of an incoming message from Gul Dukat, the former Cardassian administrator of Bajor. Sisko's office was originally Dukat's. O'Brien notes that the Cardassians are quick to reappear right after the Enterprise has departed.

Dukat and his officers come on board, and they are an arrogant lot. Whereas the Klingons may be the Mongols of space, the Cardassians are probably the closest thing to Nazis that the Twenty-Fourth Century has to offer. Conversing in the office, Sisko and Dukat are wary, barely concealing their mutual hostility behind a strained exterior of exaggerated good manners. This is oddly reminiscent of the briefing between Sisko and Picard, except that what Gul Dukat wishes to express is a thinly veiled threat. He is aware of Sisko's visit to Kai Opaka, and inquires innocently about the Orb. Sisko denies all knowledge of any Orb. Dukat knows he's lying, and Sisko really has no intention of deceiving him. The lie serves merely as a curt means of turning down Dukat's offer of "assistance." With this interview over, Dukat returns to his warship, but his officers remain behind to enjoy themselves on the newly restored Promenade which they themselves probably helped to demolish less than a week before.

Sisko makes his way to Jadzia Dax's laboratory to inquire about her progress in her studies of the Orb and its history. She tells him of the Denorios Belt, a charged plasma field that is a major navigational threat. She has learned of an incident, two centuries earlier, in which a predecessor of Kai Opaka, known as Kai Taluno, was stranded in that region of space for two days. during that time he had a rather unusual experience in which, in his words, "the heavens opened and swallowed his vessel."

(The original draft of the pilot script features a few lines of dialogue, cut from the shooting script, in which Dax reveals that she actually met Kai Taluno briefly in one of her previous Trill lives.)

The Denorios Belt, she goes on, is the location where most of the Orbs were found, and it is also an area marked by occasional but consistent reports of heavy neutrino activity.

(Another line cut from the original draft makes note of an infant shapeshifter of unknown species found adrift in a spacecraft in the Denorios Belt over thirty years earlier— clearly a reference to Odo, although subsequently that was changed to fifty years before in Odo's basic origin.)

Dax then produces a computer generated map showing the general area in space where all these unusual occurrences seem to originate. Sisko decides that it is time to go take a closer look. But the nearby Cardassians pose a bit of a problem.

Down in Quark's establishment, the Cardassian officers are winning hand over fist at the gambling tables, when Major Kira, backed by Chief O'Brien, announces that the bar is being closed down. Quark is incensed, but Kira is adamant. Reluctant to allow the Cardassians to take away all the gold they've won, there is nothing he can do, so he has an assistant produce a sack for them to put their winnings in. Quark glances at O'Brien and the Major, suggesting that the whole scene is a massive put-on. Which in fact it is. When the Cardassians return to their ship, they place the sack in one of their lockers. As soon as they are gone, the "sack" shape-shifts, revealing that it is actually Odo.

Sisko and Dax board the runabout craft Rio Grande (in the first draft script, the Giotto) and wait. The Cardassian ship experiences a severe systems crash which cripples their shields and their sensors. The Rio Grande, now free from Cardassian observation, takes off and heads for the Denorios Belt region.

Efforts to interface with a Cardassian transporter and beam back Odo prove difficult. The equipment wont work until, in frustration, O'Brien kicks a panel on the control board and Odo beams back to Deep Space Nine.

**FIFTH ACT:
INVESTIGATING THE BELT**

In the Rio Grande, Sisko and Dax have reached their destination. Sensors detect an increase in neutrino activities outside the runabout, but levels inside the craft are mysteriously unaffected. Neutrino levels increase until there is a brilliant explosion of light and the Rio Grande is drawn into a wormhole. Everything goes haywire; Dax remains calm, while Sisko is obviously stressed out as they pass through the spectacular special effects of the wormhole and finally emerge, once more, in normal space. Sisko is astounded to discover that they have travelled to the Gamma Quadrant, seventy thousand light years away from their previous location. Dax's readings on the wormhole indicate that it may actually be the first truly stable wormhole ever discovered.

Turning the ship around, Sisko and Dax enter the wormhole once more, hoping for a safe and simple journey back. The ship loses velocity inside the wormhole, slows down, and finally lands on some unseen and unknown surface.

**SIXTH ACT:
STRANDED IN THE WORMHOLE**

Sensors indicate an atmosphere as well— but where are they? Sisko grabs his phaser and is first out the hatch, finding himself facing a dark, stormy scene of rugged rock faces. Dax follows but she sees herself and Sisko in an idyllic garden setting. They don't quite have time to figure out the obvious disparity in their perceptions before they both see another Orb approaching. It probes them with a green beam, and suddenly Sisko finds the stony ground beneath him beginning to crack until all semblance of a solid surface is gone, and he is lost in an endless expanse of light.

Dax, meanwhile, is completely enveloped by the green light of the Orb, which draws her into it and then hurtles off into space.

Back at Deep Space Nine, where Major Kira and Chief O'Brien are desperately scanning for any sign of the Rio Grande, sensors suddenly detect the Orb as it emerges from the wormhole. On Kira's orders, O'Brien beams the Orb aboard only to see it disappear, leaving Jadzia Dax standing on the Ops Center deck.

Alone in the white light that surrounds him, Sisko is subjected to sudden flashes of images, beginning with the scene of Jennifer on the beach and including such persons as Locutus/Picard, Kai Opaka, and himself.

Sisko's attempts to speak with whoever (or whatever) is subjecting him to this seem futile, until the image of the beach scene holds, and he is there with Jennifer again. Except it is only an image of her, with the unknown alien presence speaking through it. But it seems absolutely real to Sisko. Throughout their interaction, the alien mind "tries on" various forms— Picard, Kai Opaka, the Bolan from the Saratoga— and Jake at the fishing hole.

It is while conversing with this form that Sisko realizes the communications challenge he is faced with. The aliens have no concept of linear time. For it (or them) all existence is simultaneous.

Back on Deep Space Nine, Dax expresses the opinion that the wormhole may not be a natural phenomenon, but a created artifact. These ruminations are interrupted by O'Brien's announcement that Gul Dukat is moving his ship toward the wormhole; obviously, the Cardassian sensors are back on line.

Kira, realizing the importance that the wormhole might have for Bajor's devastated economy, asks O'Brien if it would be possible to move the space station away from Bajor and closer to the wormhole. O'Brien thinks it is absolutely impossible, but an idea tossed out by Dax sets him to thinking. Perhaps he can modify the deflectors and form a field around the space station that will lower its inertial mass, which will enable him to use its six thrusters in order to move the station. . . maybe. (This, by the way, has to be one of the classic examples of scientific Trekspeak ever perpetrated on a television audience!) Meanwhile, a call is put out to the Enterprise, which is still a mere two days away.

Leaving O'Brien to work this sticky problem out, Major Kira takes Doctor Bashir along on a mission to rescue Sisko. Odo, keen to get into the area where he was discovered, goes along too, as he believes the secret of his origin may lie on the other side of the wormhole.

SEVENTH ACT: THE STRUGGLE CONTINUES

Meanwhile, Sisko's struggles to communicate continue. Taking the forms of Picard and Locutus, the alien mind considers destroying Sisko and his kind as dangerous and destructive creatures. A 1920's-era ball player (described as Ty Cobb in the script) also appears, the alien mind having tapped into Sisko's love of baseball, and joins that particular chorus.

Sisko counters this by claiming that he was sent by the people that the aliens had tried to contact with their Orbs but the aliens refute this. They sought creatures like themselves, not disturbing corporeal beings with bizarre notions about linear time. Sisko tries to explain that in order understand his kind, the aliens must understand the importance of experience to humans and their ilk— and is once again faced with explaining linear time. The aliens seem perturbed by the notion of future time— the idea of something not yet existing obviously bothers them.

After some rough starts, and near disaster, O'Brien succeeds in creating the desired field around the Deep Space Nine station. The station begins its journey to the wormhole. In the runabout Yang-Tse K'ien, Major Kira hails the Cardassian ship. But Gul Dukat, playing the game instigated by Sisko's disavowal

of the Orb, pretends to know nothing of any wormhole. Kira tries to convince Gul Dukat that the wormhole is too dangerous to enter, but the Cardassian thinks she's bluffing, and will not listen to her.

Taking the form of Jennifer, the aliens whisk Sisko away to a picnic scene in a wooded glen, which we discover is the time and place where Sisko and Jennifer decided to have a child. They observe the scene, enacted by another Ben and Jennifer, as the aliens try to understand. Suddenly they are back on the Saratoga, at the scene of Jennifer's death. The aliens sense that this is a crucial element in comprehending Sisko, but still don't understand it. Suddenly, the scene begins to vanish, and the Jennifer-alien, and the dead Jennifer, all fade away as Sisko once again finds himself in the brilliant white void.

Back in space, Kira and her crew witness the passage of the Cardassian warship into the wormhole. It promptly collapses and disappears in a blinding flash.

**EIGHTH ACT:
CARDASSIANS CAN'T WAIT**

On Deep Space Nine, Dax and O'Brien are dumbfounded as sensors indicate that the wormhole has ceased to exist. The good news is, the space station will catch up with the Yang-Tse K'ien in about three hours. The bad news is that the Cardassians are wondering what has happened to Gul Dukat's vessel. O'Brien, aware of the danger this presents, is nonetheless amused by the fact that, if the wormhole does not reappear, it will take Gul Dukat nearly seventy years to return to Cardassian territory. In the meanwhile, his fellow Cardassians are growing impatient with Kira's refusal to answer their questions.

In his limbo of light, Sisko is apprised of the situation by his hosts. As they feared, he has led more of his kind to the wormhole. With the warlike Cardassians impinging on their world, the aliens have discontinued the wormhole as a defensive measure. They regard physical beings like Sisko as a threat. They have no regard for the consequences of their actions. Sisko seizes upon this point. A key element of his linear lifestyle is the awareness that his acts do have consequences. So far, all he has shown the aliens is that humans and their kind don't know what those consequences will be. Sisko accepts this, but points out that humans can use their past experience to make judgements about the future. As the alien's images shift back and forth, Sisko finally seems to be making some progress in justifying the ways of man to the aliens. But he finds himself back in his ravaged quarters on board the doomed Saratoga. The aliens have tapped into his deepest secret. Despite all he has said about past, future and the passage of linear time, to their probing intelligence he really exists there, at the scene of his wife's death.

Meanwhile, the Cardassians, grown tired of waiting for explanations, have sent three of their warships to pry an explanation out of Major Kira, who has returned to Deep Space Nine following its arrival near the wormhole site. Kira has O'Brien throw up a thoron field to block the Cardassian sensors just in time to keep them from discovering the space station's minimal defenses.

The Cardassian commander, Gul Jasad, is less than responsive to the explanation he finally gets from Major Kira. For one thing, there is no sign of the wormhole into which she claims Gul Dukat's vessel has vanished. As far as Jasad is concerned, Kira is simply lying. His ships begin to power up their phasers.

NINTH ACT: THE FINAL FACEDOWN

The Cardassians flood the area with lepton interference as well, blocking any communication with Starfleet, and Gul Jasal demands the immediate surrender of Deep Space Nine. When Major Kira asks for a day to prepare, Gul Jasal haughtily gives her an hour in which to comply. Chief O'Brien points out that being taken prisoner by Cardassians is one of the least pleasant prospects in the known universe.

Sisko is again reliving the death of his wife Jennifer, as the Jennifer alien watches. He tries to save her again, but to no avail. The aliens finally begin to understand that linear existence ends, and that this must be a great trauma to Sisko's kind. As they begin to understand Sisko, they finally help him understand that there are some things in his mode of perception that echo their own means of existence: his constant mental return to the traumatic scene of his wife's violent death is not linear, so Sisko begins to understand the aliens as well. He can finally accept his wife's death. A tentative communication between two alien races has finally been established.

Meanwhile, O'Brien has been busy setting up an illusion that will give the Cardassians pause when they penetrate the thoron field: the illusion that Deep Space Nine has been heavily armed since the Cardassian withdrawal. On Kira's orders, he fires six photon torpedos (all they have) at the lead Cardassian vessel.

When Gul Jasad hails Major Kira, she claims that the station is armed. While she admits she might be bluffing, she points out that as a Bajoran, she really has nothing to lose, especially not in a battle with Cardassians. Gul Jasad is surprised to discover that his sensors indicate that the space station has five thousand photon torpedos and a full array of phasers on board. Jasad is positive that this is all some sort of illusion. Can he risk being wrong? He sends for reinforcements but decides to test DS9's defenses. He fires on the station, shaking it all over and causing considerable damage. O'Brien lets loose with a boosted phaser blast which does some damage to a Cardassian ship, but the attack continues. Shields begin to drop under the Cardassian barrage, and the situation seems hopeless. All the DS9 crew can do is instigate evacuation procedures and tend to the wounded. Doctor Bashir reveals that despite his faults he is a good doctor.

Suddenly, a flash of light reveals that the wormhole has returned, and the Rio Grand emerges, leading the missing Cardassian warship out. With this revelation the battle ends, much to Gul Jasad's disappointment.

Some time later, things have finally settled down. Deep Space Nine is now in place as the gateway to the wormhole, as the aliens have decided to allow linear, corporeal beings to use it for access to the Gamma quadrant. The planet Bajor, administering the wormhole with Federation backup, is now in a perfect position for economic recovery. Even the Cardassians, unwilling to cross the Federation, are friendly with the Bajoran people now. (In the original draft of the script, they even return the stolen Orbs to Bajor.)

Even so, there is still a lot of work to be done. Sisko now wants the job, and tells this to Captain Picard. Picard, has not even gotten around to that task yet, and he and Sisko part on much more agreeable terms than before. He can see that Sisko has been changed by his experience in the wormhole. The Enterprise departs, and work begins, as the first ships begin to approach Deep Space Nine on their way to explore the wormhole.

"PAST PROLOGUE"

The episode begins with Doctor Julian Bashir sitting at a table in a quiet corner of the Promenade, drinking a glass of tea. He is approached by a Cardassian named Garek, a rather unctuous individual who makes Bashir nervous. Garek, who owns a clothing shop in the Promenade, claims he merely wants to be friends with Bashir. Clearly uncomfortable, Bashir tells Garek he's heard rumors that, as the last Cardassian left on Deep Space Nine, Garek is a spy of sorts for his government. Garek laughs this off, and invites Bashir to drop by his shop any time.

Once Garek has gone, Bashir can barely contain his excitement, and he rushes to Ops to tell a largely disinterested O'Brien of his encounter with the "spy." Sisko points out that there is no proof that Garek is a spy, but Bashir can't believe that there isn't some hidden significance to their encounter, and even asks if O'Brien can rig some sort of monitoring device for the doctor to wear— which exasperates O'Brien and amuses Dax.

This banter is interrupted when Major Kira announces that a Cardassian warship is pursuing a smaller craft into Bajoran space. Attempts to hail the intruding Cardassians are ignored, but audio contact with the Bajoran vessel is established when its sole occupant asks for emergency docking. But sensors indicate that the small craft is coming apart, and O'Brien beams the pilot off the craft just before it explodes.

The injured man is about to be hustled off to the infirmary, but has time to identify himself as Tana Los and to ask for political asylum— just before recognizing Major Kira.

We discover that Major Kira and Tana fought together in the Bajoran resistance. After Tana is taken to have his injuries attended to by Doctor Bashir, Sisko receives a message from Gul Danar, the commanding officer of the

Cardassian ship. The Cardassians regard Tana Los as a dangerous criminal and want Sisko to hand him over. Sisko won't do this, although he has yet to decide on the asylum issue. Instead, he gives the Cardassians permission to dock, and orders Dax to use every bit of available bureaucratic red tape to delay that docking.

Major Kira insists that Sisko give Tana Los asylum. When pressed by Sisko, she reluctantly admits that Tana was a member of one of Bajor's most extreme terrorist groups. Major Kira herself was never a member of this group, which the provisional government of Bajor itself regards as undesirable, but feels that a man like Tana still has a place in the rebuilding of Bajoran society.

Major Kira and Sisko visit Tana in the infirmary, where Bashir is amazed at the many terrible scars on Tana's body. Sisko questions Tana and still has not announced a decision about granting him asylum. Sisko leaves; Major Kira stays behind and continues to converse with Tana, who is surprised to find that she's a Major. He questions her loyalty, she questions his group's continued violence against the Cardassians. Unable to answer her, he admits that he's tired of all the violence.

Determined to win asylum for Tana, Major Kira goes over Commander Sisko's head and contacts the female Admiral Rollman at Starfleet to complain of Sisko's handling of the situation.

As the Cardassian docking procedures continue, Chief O'Brien approaches Sisko and reminds him of how the Cardassians treat their prisoners. O'Brien wouldn't turn his worst enemy over to the Cardassians. Sisko receives a subspace message from Starfleet. It seems that Admiral Rollman wasn't too happy at having Major Kira interrupt an important meeting. Sisko isn't too happy to find out about it, either.

When Major Kira visits Tana again, he gives her a hard time about her loyalties, and suggests that she's forgotten her days as a fighter.

Sisko, meanwhile, meets with Gul Danar, the Cardassian captain, who is angry at the long time it took to dock at Deep Space Nine. Sisko counters by placing the blame on all the repairs necessitated by the Cardassian damage to the space station. The Cardassian insists that Sisko hand Tana over lest he commit more acts of terrorism, but Sisko decides to grant asylum instead, telling his adversary to take it up with the Bajoran provisional government at a later date. The captain storms out of Sisko's office in a bad mood, even for a Cardassian.

Major Kira escorts Tana Los, who has recovered from his most recent injuries, to private quarters, where he begins to harass her again about her new position. As a long-time Bajoran freedom fighter, he is just as opposed to having the Federation around as he was to the Cardassians. When Major Kira defends the presence of the Federation as necessary, he doesn't buy it, and he scoffs at her belief that the wormhole to the Gamma Quadrant is the key to renewed Bajoran prosperity. She tries to argue for her point of view, but it is obvious that his view of the future of Bajor is really an impossibly idealistic concept of recreating the Bajor that existed before sixty years of Cardassian occupation and exploitation. [In "Ensign Ro" it was established that there had been forty years of occupation—The Continuity Guy.] Still, he swears that he has forsworn his former terrorist group, and Major Kira is pleased to tell him that she is already talking to key Bajoran Deputies about granting him amnesty. He seems pleased at this, but after she leaves his quarters, we see an expression on his face that suggests that his true plans are not what they might seem to be.

Meanwhile, there's trouble at the disembarkation dock: two Klingon women refuse to surrender their weapons before boarding the station, and at least one security guard is down as a result of this disagreement. Odo intercedes and manages to get them to cooperate. The women in question are Lursa and Batur, the scheming sisters of Worf's late enemy Duras (they were last seen in the NEXT GENERATION episode "Redemption, Part Two").

Odo then informs Commander Sisko of the two Klingons' presence on Deep Space Nine. The Commander knows who the sisters are. The Klingon High Council has banished them as renegades. Since then, Lursa and Batur have been popping up all over the quadrant trying to get together enough money to arm themselves for another attempt to grab political power on the Klingon homeworld. Odo suggests avoiding any trouble by simply turning the two women over to the Klingons, but Sisko vetoes this idea. Better for Odo just to keep an eye on them.

Written by Kathryn Powell

Directed by Winrich Kolbe

Regular Cast:
Avery Brooks as Commander Benjamin Sisko
Rene Auberjonois as Odo
Siddig El Fadil as Doctor Bashir
Terry Farrell as Lieutenant Dax
Cirroc Lofton as Jake Sisko
Colm Meaney as Chief O'Brien
Armin Shimerman as Quark
Nana Visitor as Major Kira

Guest Stars:
Jeffrey Nordling
Andrew Robinson
Gwynyth Walsh
Barabara March
Susan Bay
Vaughn Armstrong
Richard Ryder: Bajoran Deputy

The Klingon sisters have taken up a solitary table on an upper level of Quark's establishment. It's a busy time at the bar, and everyone is there including Garek. Playing sleuth, Doctor Bashir joins Garek at his table. The chatty Cardassian offers some comments on Klingon fashions as a means of pointing out Lursa and Batur. Just as quickly, he draws Bashir's attention to the arrival of Tana Los. The Klingons spot Tana also, and rise from their table, following him out of the bar.

Meeting Tana Los in an isolated storage area, the impatient Klingons waste no time in getting to the point.

Tana has promised them a large sum of money, and they're getting awfully tired of waiting for it. He assures them that the cash is on the way, and they part company. But the Klingons make a friendly death threat against Tana, promising unpleasant consequences if he does not come through as promised.

After this little tete-a-tete breaks up, a rat sitting in a nearby corner begins to grow and change shape, revealing that it is really Odo, who has witnessed the entire exchange.

Major Kira, meanwhile, has been busy seeking amnesty for Tana Los and is on the verge of having a sufficient number of Bajoran deputies ready to agree to the deal. Major Kira thanks Commander Sisko for his assistance in this effort. Sisko responds by hoping that she'll show her gratitude by resisting any future urge to go over his head and contact the Admiral again.

After this exchange, Odo arrives and informs Sisko of the scene he has just witnessed between Tana and the Duras sisters. They both wonder what the Klingons are selling to Tana, but Sisko has a pretty good hunch where the money is coming from. He's sure that the two ex-terrorists coming in to join Tana Los in his alleged plea for amnesty are actually bringing the cash for Tana. And the complications in this situation have left Sisko wondering just how far he can trust Kira.

Meanwhile, the two surly Klingon women are visiting Garek in his shop. They have an offer to make to the Cardassian government through Garek— once their business with Tana Los is concluded, they would like to sell the terrorist to the Cardassians, if the price is right. He punches out a price on a small computer pad. The women are offended by the offer, but he assures them he's prepared to negotiate.

Major Kira, meanwhile, has informed Tana that the amnesty deal is almost guaranteed. But he cannot help his urge to criticize her present position vis-a-vis the Federation, and it soon dawns on Kira that he knew all about her presence on Deep Space Nine before he ever came there. He admits what she fears the most: he has not renounced his cause. But, he assures her, his new plan to win Bajor for the Bajorans will not entail any violence. All he needs now is for Kira to provide him with a small craft capable of warp speed. This request seriously compromises Kira's loyalties.

Garek corners Doctor Bashir again and tells Julian that he must come to his shop and buy a new suit at precisely 20:55 hours. When Bashir doesn't get the hint, Garek repeats his "request" and makes a point of stressing the importance of the time. Bashir rushes to Sisko to tell him of this development. Commander Sisko muses that Garek may be trying to tell him that the Federation and the Cardassians are facing a situation where they have some common ground. Possibly information the Cardassians could not relay through the usual channels without serious loss of face. His conclusion: Bashir could use a new suit.

Kira turns to Odo for advice, and finally decides to tell Sisko about Tana Los' request for a runabout.

Bashir is late for his "fitting" at Garek's, and the Cardassian merchant barely has enough time to conceal the doctor in a dressing cubicle before the two Klingon women arrive to finalize the deal with the Cardassians. They are going to meet the Bajoran near one of the moons of Bajor Eight and sell him a cylinder of bi-dyttrium. Once the Klingons leave the scene, the Cardassians can have him.

As soon as the coast is clear, Bashir steps out, full of questions. He asks Garek what bi-dyttrium is. Garek replies that it is a very powerful energy source. When used in conjunction with an anti-matter converter, it becomes an explosive device of incredible power. The reason the Cardassians were chasing Tana Los was because he had just stolen an anti-matter converter from them! Soon Tana will have an unspeakably potent bomb in his possession.

Doctor Bashir and Major Kira join Commander Sisko and the other officers in Ops to discuss the situation. Technically, having an anti-matter converter is not in itself a crime, but once Tana Los has the bi-dyttrium as well, he can be arrested. Sisko decides to let Kira give Tana the runabout and capture him after he completes his deal with the Klingons. Kira volunteers to go along with Tana, but Sisko vetoes this idea until the Major points out that if she stays behind, Tana will be certain to suspect that something is amiss.

And so, Tana Los and Major Kira take off in the runabout Yang-Tse K'ien. While they make their way to the rendezvous with the Klingons, Tana rigs up the anti-matter converter. Meanwhile, Commander Sisko and Chief O'Brien have already taken the runabout Ganges to a concealed position near the rendezvous point. The Klingons appear and beam over to the Yang-Tse K'ien, trade the bi-dyttrium for the money, beam back to their ship and go on their way while Tana adds this final ingredient to his bomb.

Sisko, in the Ganges heads to intercept Tana, and Gul Danar's Cardassian warship also converges on the terrorist. Detecting both vessels, Tana realizes that he's been set up both by the Klingons and by Major Kira. Tana attacks Kira and gets her phaser. He then orders her to take the runabout on a warp-speed course for Deep Space Nine. If she won't obey, he'll detonate the bomb at their current location, releasing deadly radiation that will kill the inhabitants of the nearest planet. Kira complies. Sisko threatens to fire on the craft but he can't. At warp speed a direct hit would simply spread the same radiation over a vast area of space.

Major Kira curses Tana for a liar; he'd promised her that no one would be hurt, but now he's going to blow up

Deep Space Nine, killing everyone on board the station. But this, he reveals, is not his plan. He intends to enter the wormhole and detonate the device just inside it. This will destroy the Bajoran end of the passage to the Gamma Quadrant.

They encounter turbulence as they enter the wormhole, causing Tana to drop his guard. Kira struggles with him; soon enough, he gets the drop on her again with the phaser, but by that time they've passed through the wormhole and are in normal space again. The Ganges, bearing Sisko and O'Brien, comes through next, and Sisko orders Tana to surrender. When Tana stalls, Sisko asks him if he'd rather surrender to the Cardassian ship that should be coming through the wormhole next? Tana reluctantly hands the phaser over to Kira.

Back on Deep Space Nine, Tana is taken into custody. As he is carried away, Kira tries to explain her actions to him. He will never understand, and calls her a traitor.

"A MAN ALONE"

The episode opens with Doctor Bashir walking in on Jadzia Dax, who is meditating. A suspended globe of swirling colors is in the air; the object of this computer-assisted mental exercise is to use the mind's energy to turn the lobe a single, solid color, which even Dax has not yet achieved after one hundred and forty years of effort. Bashir tries to flirt with Dax, and goes along when she steers him into trying his hand at the Sphere— which promptly dissolves as soon as he takes control of it. Dax chides him for having other things on his mind. Commander Sisko arrives and invites Dax to dinner, leaving a flustered Julian in the lurch.

In Quark's establishment, Odo can't help but overhear a rather heated argument between Miles and Keiko O'Brien. In fact, neither can anyone else in the bar, even though the couple is seated at a table on the upper level. The shapeshifter is rather bemused by human relationships, which he admits. Quark is stunned to learn that Odo has never "coupled." Since Odo is the only known member of his species, he could never properly mate until another member of his species is discovered. [This raises a number of interesting questions regarding this subject. One can only imagine that the reproductive activities of a species that is an amorphous protoplasmic mass might not be a lot of fun. And what gender, if any, is Odo in "his" natural state? On the other hand, if Odo were interested in sex strictly for recreational purposes, he'd probably be very popular with species posing no barrier. Will Deep Space Nine tackle any of these dubious questions? Only time will tell!]

Sisko and Dax arrive, a fact quickly noted by the libidinous Quark, who shares Doctor Bashir's interest in her, but is less subtle about it. Bashir isn't very subtle, anyway. The key difference here is that Bashir's interest is given an added twist by the fact that Dax is a Trill. Where many other people would be put off by the fact that this beautiful woman shares her body with an ancient

slug, Quark obviously does not care about that. He probably wouldn't care if she had thirty-seven different personalities, as long as the external package was well-designed.

While Dax and Sisko talk about the old days, and Keiko walks out on Miles O'Brien, Odo recognizes a Bajoran at one of the gambling tables. Confronting the gambler, Odo gives him twenty-six hours to get off the space station; the two men scuffle briefly until Sisko breaks the fight up.

Meanwhile, in a passageway outside the Promenade, O'Brien catches up with his wife, and they have a conversation that is taken directly from the first draft of the script for the pilot episode, "Emissary." Keiko is concerned about their future; she doesn't feel that this grim space station is a good place for them to raise their daughter. Furthermore, she herself feels out of place, as there seems to be little use for a botanist on board Deep Space Nine. (This dialogue originally took place on board the Enterprise just before Miles O'Brien disembarked, a scene cut from the pilot.) O'Brien is called away to look into a power grid problem, leaving Keiko alone.

Meanwhile, Jake Sisko encounters the Ferengi boy, Nog, and tries to befriend him. (This scene was also originally part of the first draft script for "Emissary." Although "A Man Alone" was the third DEEP SPACE NINE episode aired, the evidence of this scene and the one preceding, as well as the scenes of Sisko and Dax getting reacquainted, suggests that "A Man Alone" was probably the second episode produced.)

At the Commander's behest, Odo explains his actions to Sisko. The man in the Promenade was Ibodan, a Bajoran black marketeer, and a murderer. Odo recalls how Ibodan allowed a child to die because the child's parents could not afford to purchase a life-saving medicine from him. Ibodan also killed a Cardassian, a crime for which Odo arrested him. Ibodan received a life sentence under the Cardassians, but now the Bajoran provisional government has set him free. Odo still seems to regard the man as the lowest sort of criminal and is determined to get him off Deep Space Nine by any means, an attitude Sisko finds somewhat disturbing.

Some time later, Ibodan is in a Holosuite, being massaged by an alien woman. Events seem as though they are about to reveal whether or not the Holosuites really are brothels or not, when a black-clad figure, with face unseen, interrupts the proceedings and stabs Ibodan in the back with a very large and ugly knife.

While Nog and Jake become friends, Bashir reveals a certain jealousy of Sisko; Dax counters by explaining that, while Trill host bodies might have certain desires, the composite mind tries to keep matters on a "higher plane." Their conversation is interrupted when Doctor Bashir is called to the scene of Ibodan's death.

Nog and Jake, meanwhile, are cementing their friendship by getting up to some mischief. Hiding behind a grill in the Promenade, they release some sort of tiny alien insects from a small box; two Bajoran diners, attacked by the all-but-invisible creatures, suddenly find themselves itching all over—and then their skin color begins to shift, cycling though a number of bright hues, much like Elmer Fudd losing his temper in a Bugs Bunny cartoon. Panic turns to embarrassment when the effect wears off and the Bajoran couple returns to normal. Nog and Jake, beside themselves with laughter, suddenly find themselves being hauled off by a Security Officer. Keiko O'Brien observes this and begins thinking.

At the murder scene, the evidence is puzzling. The door to the Holosuite had only opened twice: once when Ibodan checked in, and again thirteen minutes later, when someone (presumably the killer) left. The woman was part of the Holosuite-program so there was no witness to the crime. Could the murderer have entered with Ibodan? There was no beam-in or out, so that possibility is dismissed. The actual murder was clean and precise: the killer obviously knew Bajoran anatomy well enough to slide the blade neatly between his victim's ribs. Baffled by all this, Sisko orders Doctor Bashir to do a DNA scan of the Holosuite.

Another Bajoran provides some information: some time before his murder, Ibodan had told this man that he was afraid that he would be killed by Odo.

Teleplay: Michael Piller
Story by Gerald Sanford and Michael Piller

Directed by Paul Lynch

Regular Cast:
Avery Brooks as Commander Benjamin Sisko
Rene Auberjonois as Odo
Siddig El Fadil as Doctor Bashir
Terry Farrell as Lieutenant Dax
Cirroc Lofton as Jake Sisko
Colm Meaney as Chief O'Brien
Armin Shimerman as Quark
Nana Visitor as Major Kira

Guest Stars:
Rosalind Chao
Edward Lawrence Albert
Max Grodenchik
Peter Vogt
Aron Eisenerg
Stephen James Carver
Tom Klunis
Scott Trost: Bajoran Officer
Patrick Cupo: Bajoran Man
Kathryn Graf: Bajoran Woman
Hana Hatae: Molly
Diana Cignoni: Dabo Girl
Judy Durand: Computer Voice

Odo, meanwhile, investigates Ibodan's quarters on board the ship that brought him to Deep Space Nine. He finds it interesting that Ibodan had chosen a room with two bunks, even though the ship's records show that Ibodan had been traveling alone. And Ibodan's personal computer notes indicate that his visit to the station had something to do with the security chief.

Keiko O'Brien approaches Sisko with an idea: why not let her start a school for the dozen or so children on board Deep Space Nine? Sisko finds this an interesting idea and promises to give her the supplies she needs. Jake will attend, but Sisko is very angry about Jake's antics and refuses to allow him to see Nog any more.

Bashir reviews the results of his DNA scan for the rest of the officers: apparently, Ibodan was the only person to have been in the Holosuite. Of course, the scan was done too late to exclude Bashir, Sisko, Kira or Odo from its results. Musing out loud, Odo can't imagine how the killer could have gained entrance to the Holosuite—except, maybe, if he were a shapeshifter. The rest of the officers glance at each other uneasily at this prospect.

Alone with Major Kira, Odo states that someone is obviously trying to frame him for Ibodan's murder. His only alibi: he was in his natural state in a bucket in his office at the time of the murder. Odo must return to this form every eighteen hours; obviously, the killer knew this, too. Unfortunately, Odo can think of at least five hundred people who'd be happy to do this to him. He contacts Doctor Bashir and asks him to do a sweep of Ibodan's quarters.

Nog's father (the gambling pit boss, and Quark's brother) doesn't like the school idea when Keiko presents it to him. Ferengi education is largely a sink-or-swim introduction to the world of commerce. Keiko admits that she can't give the boy a Ferengi education. But if she can teach him about other worlds and cultures, he might have an advantage over other Ferengi in doing business with those cultures. This gives Nog's father pause for thought, but he's still not convinced. After all, Ferengi are not taught by women. But, he'll give the idea some consideration.

Elsewhere in the Promenade, the Bajoran who earlier linked Odo with the murder is discussing the case with some other Bajorans at Quark's bar. He's obviously trying to stir up sentiment against Odo. He is quick to point out that Odo served as DS9 security chief under the Cardassians, and hints at collaboration. Quark speaks up to defend Odo against this charge: sure, he might be the Ferengi's worst enemy, but that's because he's honest, and even Quark sees that Odo would never have collaborated with the Cardassians. But the angry Bajorans are not convinced. And at the end of the bar, a hooded older Bajoran with a white beard looks on with quiet interest.

Doctor Bashir does a sweep of Ibodan's quarters and finds some interesting fragments near a waste disposal unit.

Commander Sisko, meanwhile, has been asked by the Bajorans on Deep Space Nine to relieve Odo of his duties. Kira objects to this; she sees this as an unwarranted persecution of the redoubtable security chief. But the conflict of interest inherent in having a suspect in a murder case as the investigator in charge of that case forces Sisko's hand, and he places Kira and Dax in charge of the investigation.

Back in his lab, Doctor Bashir determines that the fragments that he's found are pieces of a biological sample container, and that there are still some vestiges of organic matter on them. A closer look reveals DNA fragments;

Bashir sets up a bioregenerative field, hoping to discover just what it was that Ibodan was up to. (This writer figured the whole story out at this point— how about you, fellow sleuths?)

Odo returns from his dismissal by Sisko to find his office has been vandalized. Quark shows up and offers to find out who did it, but Odo passes on this offer. Quark admits that he'll miss his adversary. In the midst of their usual bickering, Odo surprises Quark by asking the Ferengi if he could find any use for a shapeshifter in his line of work. Quark thinks about this for a moment; the movement of the gears of his brain are almost visible on his face as he thinks of the possibilities this would offer. Suddenly, he realizes that Odo is putting him on! Still, he has found out something that might be of interest to Odo: Quark knows which Bajorans Ibodan spent most of his time with when he was in a Cardassian prison.

In Bashir's lab, the organic matter he discovered is growing into something, but the DNA patterns keep shifting and he cannot tell what exactly it is going to grow into.

Later, at lunch with Sisko, Bashir inquires about the Commander's relationship with Dax. Sisko reassures Bashir that they are just friends, but cautions the young doctor that Trills often have different ideas about romance than humans.

When Odo goes to the bar, all the Bajorans leave, followed a moment later by the ever-present Lurian. As Odo makes his way to his office, he is followed by an angry mob, which stands outside his office making threatening noises. O'Brien sees all this and alerts Sisko to send in security.

The crowd becomes more restless, and only gets worse when Major Kira shows up with security.

Meanwhile, Bashir has determined that the chromosome patterns for the form growing in his lab are distinctly humanoid, and he guesses the truth of the matter.

Sisko reaches the mob scene and orders the crowd to disperse; they're just about ready to lynch Odo. (Just how they plan to do this isn't exactly clear; a creature like Odo could easily escape them as long as the special effects budget for the episode holds up. . .) There's a bit of a scuffle but Security holds firm, and Major Kira knocks some sense into one member of the mob foolish enough to cross her. But the mob's leader demands that they hand Odo over, as they have enough evidence to convince them of his guilt in the murder of Ibodan.

At this moment, Doctor Bashir arrives and announces new evidence: the murder victim was not Ibodan!

Back in the lab, he reveals that he has just about finished growing a clone of Ibodan. That was why Ibodan needed a room with two bunks: he cloned himself, and then murdered the clone to frame Odo.

The bearded Bajoran, meanwhile, makes his way back to Ibodan's quarters in a hurry. He doesn't notice a chair that wasn't there before. The chair metamorphosizes into Odo, who pulls the beard off the man, revealing the face of Ibodan. While in prison, Ibodan had spent a lot of time with some cloning specialists, and picked up the knowledge that would enable him to pursue his plan for revenge by cloning himself. Killing a clone is still murder, of course, and Ibodan is arrested and turned over to the Bajorans. This time, he won't be getting out any time soon. As for the second clone: it will soon join Bajoran society.

Finally, Keiko O'Brien opens her school. At first, no one shows up, except Jake. Then Nog shows up, brought by his father, who has decided to try the school— for a while.

"BABEL"

Chief O'Brien has been working overtime. It seems that everything on Deep Space Nine is breaking down all at once. Half a dozen angry people have been waiting in an airlock for over an hour while O'Brien attends to the jammed door. To make matters worse, an alien ship's captain, Captain Jahil, gives him a hard time regarding the delays in repairs to his ship's vessel. If he doesn't leave soon, his cargo will spoil.

Dax calls the overworked O'Brien to her lab, where some sort of power output problem has everything going haywire. O'Brien manages to get things going, then heads for Ops to fix Major Kira's navigation computer. O'Brien is by this time ready to collapse, but Sisko, not noticing this, complains about the coffee in the replicator. O'Brien lets loose with a stream of sarcasm, but still goes to fix the replicator. After spending some time lying on his side, halfway inside the device's service panel, he reactivates the replicator. There is a peculiar power surge, but then everything seems to go back to normal, and the coffee tastes okay to him now. He goes on about his business without giving it a second thought. Inside the replicator's inner workings we see a small device, obviously not a part of the replicator, begin to function.

On the Promenade, business is almost nonexistent, thanks to the lack of functioning replicators. Odo is just about the only customer in Quark's establishment, and he's there just to aim a few jibes at the Ferengi. The only other patron, a large, surly alien, is eating some stew. He's dissatisfied with it, and forces Quark to eat some of it. Quark is angry at O'Brien; the replicators on Command Level are back on line, but Quark's problems are low on O'Brien's crowded waiting list. After Odo leaves Quark accesses the computer and, overriding security codes, learns the locations of all working replicators on board Deep Space Nine.

Up in Ops, Sisko commends O'Brien on the quality of the replicator's improved coffee output. O'Brien, meanwhile, complains that he's feeling hot, and wonders whether the climate control is going bad again. As O'Brien turns to go, Sisko compliments him on Keiko's new school, and says that his son Jake really likes it. O'Brien replies, "She's flower units about the latter self." Perplexed, Sisko asks O'Brien to repeat himself; equally perplexed, O'Brien says "She's quite fond of the lad herself." Sisko seems to think that he must of mis-heard O'Brien. . . but he's not entirely certain.

On the Promenade, Quark is back in business. Dax, bemused by the attention she's getting from men, tells Major Kira that it's been eighty years since she'd been female; Kira seems less than impressed by Dax's "problem." Quark tries to invite them to his party, but they have duties elsewhere. Quark, it seems, is celebrating the "repair' of his replicators.

O'Brien is looking more and more fatigued. Kira comments on this, then jokingly tells O'Brien that one of the turbolifts is malfunctioning again. When she explains that it was just a joke, O'Brien turns to her and says: "Major, lark's true pepper."

When she tells him that she doesn't understand him, he becomes agitated: "Let birds go further loose, maybe." Nothing he says makes any sense whatsoever— obviously distressed, the Chief leaves Ops as the entire staff stares at his departure.

In the infirmary, Doctor Bashir looks O'Brien over. Everything seems normal with all his physical symptoms, but O'Brien cannot communicate, and doesn't understand what anyone says. It seems to be some sort of aphasia, a condition that leaves the thought processes unaffected but in essence redirects all aural and visual stimuli. The mystery is: Why? Aphasia is usually the aftereffect of a stroke or a severe injury to the head, and neither of these things have happened to O'Brien. He seems to be in perfect health, at least as long as he keeps his mouth shut.

Calling a staff meeting, Commander Sisko assigns Major Kira to double-check O'Brien's recent duty logs, and assigns O'Brien's duties to Jadzia Dax— but Dax is suddenly speaking nonsense herself, succumbing to the aphasia right before everyone's eyes.

Doctor Bashir intensifies his investigation, and discovers that the problem is a virus that mimics aphasia by affecting the temporal lobes of the victims and randomly re-routing neural impulses. More crew members are brought to see the doctor, spouting nonsense; the problem is spreading.

Odo questions Quark's renewed business. Quark claims that Rom repaired the replicators but Odo isn't buying that explanation. A while later, we see Quark wheeling an empty cart into some empty quarters on Command

Level, where he proceeds to fill his latest round of orders using the replicators. Much to the Ferengi's chagrin, the cart transforms itself into Odo. "I thought the front wheels were sticking a bit," he muses, caught in the act again. Odo points out that attributing the replicator "repair" to Rom was a mistake, as that particular Ferengi is not exactly intelligent.

This leads to further revelations for Sisko. The virus seems to be limited to food replicated by replicators on Command Level. But thanks to Quark's little scam, the problem affects more than one level. O'Brien's last job was a replicator adjustment. Could something be wrong with the replicators' bio-filters? How can it be fixed?

This concern is rendered moot when Bashir makes a terrible announcement: the virus has mutated, and is now air-borne, and has spread throughout the entire station. With sixty per cent of station personnel affected with the aphasia virus, Sisko imposes an absolute quarantine on Deep Space Nine.

Following the trail left in O'Brien's duty log, Major Kira locates the mysterious device in the replicator attached to the pattern generator. Obviously triggered when O'Brien reactivated the replicator, the device introduced an extra program into the replicator system on the Command Level, building the virus into all replicated food at a basic molecular level. The technology used in the device leads Major Kira to surmise that it was a sabotage device left behind by the Cardassians— but this is not correct.

Teleplay by Michael McGreevey and Naren Shankar
Story by Sally Caves and Ira Steven Behr

Directed by Paul Lynch

Regular Cast:
Avery Brooks as Commander Benjamin Sisko
Rene Auberjonois as Odo
Siddig El Fadil as Doctor Bashir
Terry Farrell as Lieutenant Dax
Cirroc Lofton as Jake Sisko
Colm Meaney as Chief O'Brien
Armin Shimerman as Quark
Nana Visitor as Major Kira

Guest Stars:
Jack Kehler
Matthew Faison
Ann Gillespie
Geraldine Farrell
Bo Zenga: Asoth
Kathleen Wirt: Aphasia Victim
Lee Brooks: Aphasia Victim
Richard Ryder: Bajoran Deputy
Frank Novak: Businessman
Todd Feder: Federation Man

Suddenly, Commander Sisko is called to the emergency hospital that has been set up to deal with the aphasia crisis, where he discovers that his son Jake has fallen prey to the virus.

Even Quark seems to have become a victim, as he is in the hospital trying to communicate with another patient with a stream of disjointed words. Even so, the basic theme of his utterances seems to be greed and acquisition. Passing by this scene, Odo cannot help but comment sarcastically, only to discover that Quark is merely checking to see if any of the customers who owe him money are faking illness. Odo comments that nobody could possibly be that devious. "I am," retorts Quark.

Meanwhile, Doctor Bashir has made some discoveries about the virus-replicating device. The virus itself is artificial: somebody actually created it. By studying all known DNA construction techniques, Bashir has determined that the virus is the work of a Bajoran scientist. (So much for Kira's theory.) The device, it seems, was part of a Bajoran underground plot. It was placed on Deep Space Nine when the station was being built eighteen years earlier. The sabotage was never implemented, for whatever reason, until O'Brien unknowingly activated the device in his efforts to provide Sisko with a decent cup of coffee. Now the question on everyone's mind is a simple but pressing one: is there an antidote?

Major Kira begins to search Bajoran records for any information on genetic scientists. One name, that of a Doctor Dekon Elig, comes up. Elig was clearly qualified to create such a virus. However, he was last seen in a Cardassian prison camp nearly a decade earlier, and his current whereabouts are unknown.

Meanwhile, O'Brien's condition is becoming progressively worse. He is running a high fever, and Bashir tells Sisko that the virus has moved on to attack O'Brien's autonomic nervous system. Seven other crew members are also in this critical state. O'Brien has only twelve hours to live. But none of Bashir's efforts to create an antidote have worked so far.

Investigating the background of Dekon Elig, Major Kira learns that Elig was killed trying to escape from the Cardassian prison camp. His death certificate is on file. Bringing up a computer display of that document, Kira notes that the certificate was witnessed and signed by a Bajoran medical assistant named Surmak Ren (is there a Bajoran named Stimpy out there somewhere as well?). But Surmak's whereabouts are also unknown ever since he was repatriated from the prison camp. Determined to find him, Kira begins a district-by-district search of Bajor.

On the Promenade, Quark is all alone playing Dabo by himself, when Odo drops by; he's just there to remind Quark that none of this would have happened if the Ferengi hadn't "stolen" replicator time from Command Level. (Not strictly true, since the virus would probably have evolved into an airborne form anyway.)

Doctor Bashir's efforts to find an antidote are cut short when he become an aphasia victim, too.

Major Kira locates Doctor Surmak Ren; he is now the head of the Ilvian medical facility. She contacts him, but as soon as she accuses him of helping Dekon Elig create the virus, he grows angry, disavows all knowledge of it, and breaks off contact.

With his staff radically diminished by the virus' effect, Sisko asks Odo to help him out in Ops. Odo seems unwilling, protesting that he is not qualified, but Sisko insists.

Major Kira breaks in on their conversation and informs Sisko of her conversation with Surmak Ren. She's convinced that he knows something, and plans to go talk to him in person. Angrily, Sisko reminds her of the quarantine— but she says that she does not plan to go to the planet. At Odo's urging, Sisko lets her go— this may be their only chance.

Soon, another crisis looms, interrupting Sisko's visit with Jake. It seems that Captain Jahil is determined to leave the station with his cargo, quarantine or no quarantine. All of his crew are in the station hospital thanks to the virus, and he intends to clear out before he catches it too.

When Sisko refuses to unlock the mooring clamps holding Jahil's ship, the Captain simply tries to break free. Reconsidering the problem, Sisko decides to retract the clamps and bring the ship back with a tractor beam— but Jahil's actions have buckled the clamps and they will not retract. Jahil's efforts have only damaged his ship, buckling its superstructure and cracking the engine core. An explosion is minutes away (of course) which will not only destroy Jahil's ship, but will also take half the docking ring with it.

Kira, in a runabout ship above Bajor, locates Surmak Ren alone in his office after hours and beams him aboard her vessel. He's furious and demands to be returned, but she sets course back for Deep Space Nine.

Back at the station, Sisko loses contact with Jahil— there's a fire on his bridge, and Jahil himself is knocked unconscious. Odo realizes that the only way to save the docking ring is to explode the mooring clamps, which must be done manually, a task the security chief volunteers for. But at this crucial moment, Sisko finally succumbs to the aphasia virus, leaving Odo alone in Ops, uncertain exactly how to proceed.

In the runabout, Surmak Ren threatens Kira with prison for kidnapping. He admits that he was present when Dekon Elig created the virus, but he was not directly involved in the project himself, and does not think that he can be any help in finding an antidote, as Dekon never mentioned one.

Kira retorts that if Surmak can't help her and the DS9 crew, then maybe he'll be more motivated to help himself. He's been exposed to the virus, too, since the moment he was beamed on board Kira's vessel.

Odo sends out a general call for help, and is dismayed when the only person to respond is his nemesis, Quark. (Earlier, Quark had advised Odo never to underestimate the Ferengi immune system.) Quark isn't exactly "volunteering", but the time to haggle over his price must wait until later. Odo needs to be beamed over to Jahil's ship. Quark assures Odo that he can do it. Just as Odo steps on the Transporter pad, Quark twists the knife: "I must have witnessed the procedure hundreds of times." But apparently, he really does know what he's doing, and Odo is transported over to the burning bridge of Jahil's freighter.

Returning to the station, Major Kira is stunned to find Quark running things. But there is no time to worry about this strange situation. She must get Surmak Ren to Bashir's lab so he can look over Bashir's work.

Facing the flames, Odo drags Captain Jahil into the airlock and races against time to set the explosives to blast the mooring clamps, all to the accompaniment of Quark broadcasting the countdown to disaster. At the last possible moment, the clamps blow, and the freighter hurtles away from the station, to explode in a blinding flash.

Working from Bashir's unfinished efforts, Surmak Ren manages to find an antidote. Normalcy is restored to the station, leaving Odo and Quark to work out the details of Quark's "hazard pay."

It's business as usual in Ops, until Sisko orders a cup of coffee from the replicator. It's gone bad again, and the Commander spits the brew out, calling out O'Brien's name in annoyance. O'Brien just raises his eyebrows sarcastically, obviously in no hurry to work on that particular replicator again.

"CAPTIVE PURSUIT"

The episode begins with Commander Sisko hearing a sexual harassment complaint from a newly signed on Dabo girl. Apparently Quark has made her aware of a provision in the Ferengi small print of her contract which obliges her to provide certain "favors" as a part of her job. Sisko assures her that such a provision will not be enforceable on Deep Space Nine, and promises her that he'll have a serious chat with Quark regarding the matter.

Suddenly, an unidentified alien ship passes through the wormhole. It seems that the first traffic from the Gamma Quadrant has finally arrived. Sisko puts the station on yellow alert (standard procedure) and scans the vessel. The spacecraft is damaged, and there is only one life form, a humanoid, on board. Hailing the craft, Sisko is answered by a green skinned, scaled individual of a reptilian cast. The ship's pilot is curious about the wormhole. He followed another ship, which Sisko assumes was a Federation patrol craft, through the "anomaly." Sisko tells the alien that his ship is damaged; they can beam him over to the space station. The alien declines to abandon his ship. O'Brien suggests that they use the tractor beam to pull the ship in to dock, so that they can help repair the damage, and the alien agrees to this course of action. The tractor beam helps to stabilize the damaged ship, and Sisko sends O'Brien, who the alien seems to trust, to greet their visitor at the airlock.

But Sisko is curious about one thing— the alien seems nervous, and he'd like to know why.

The alien ship docks, and O'Brien enters through the airlock. He finds the interior of the small craft to be quite empty. He checks with Dax in Ops and the sensor says that their guest is still there. O'Brien plays it cool, and talks reassuringly to his unseen companion as he examines the interior problems of the space vessel. Finally, while O'Brien is under what would be the dashboard of a present day car, the alien becomes visible and moves forward to join O'Brien. O'brien is alarmed and bangs his head.

The alien asks O'Brien if the engine problems can be repaired. O'Brien seems to think so, if the alien can teach him the basics of the technology. O'Brien introduces himself, by species and name, and asks the alien the same. "I am Tosk," the alien replies, an appellation which seems to serve both as his species classification and private name, as Tosk has no other term with which to describe himself. Explaining the damage to his ship, he tells O'Brien that it was caused by the turbulence of his passage through the wormhole.

O'Brien shows Tosk around the station; when they pass through a low level security field designed to detect weapons, Tosk is momentarily startled, but O'Brien sets his mind at ease. Tosk is clearly intelligent; as they pass the infirmary, he recognizes it as a "health care center." O'Brien introduces Tosk to a surprised Doctor Bashir, who is somewhat taken aback by Tosk's tendency to sniff at new acquaintances. Other activities catch Tosk's attention: Quark, kicking a cheating customer out of his gambling establishment; a Bajoran monk addressing a passer by. . . until O'Brien takes his new charge along his way to some guest quarters.

Tosk reveals that he only needs seventeen minutes of sleep per "rotation," which astounds O'Brien. Tosk also has an incredibly effective nutrient storage system in his body, and can go for long periods of time without needing to eat. O'Brien promises that they will be able to start work on Tosk's ship very soon. O'Brien leaves the quarters, and as soon as he is gone, Tosk asks the computer terminal in his new room to show him where the weapons are stored on board Deep Space Nine.

O'Brien confides to Commander Sisko that the damage to Tosk's ship was not caused by the passage through the wormhole: somebody was shooting at him. Yet despite this prevarication, O'Brien likes Tosk, and seems to feel that he poses no threat to Deep Space Nine.

Later, Tosk explains the basics of his propulsion system to O'Brien. As O'Brien had originally suspected, it uses a ramscoop which converts space matter into fuel for the ship. It should be an easy matter to replicate the needed parts, and O'Brien estimates that it should take two days at the most. Tosk seems to be in a bigger hurry than that.

O'Brien takes Tosk to Quark's place, where Tosk is surprised at O'Brien's explanation of rest and relaxation. To Tosk, it seems inconceivable that a species that already spends a whole third of its existence sleeping would need to spend even more of its time relaxing. He observes that people in the Alpha Quadrant seem to have much too much spare time on their hands.

When Quark arrives to take their order, O'Brien begins to berate the

Ferengi, explaining to Tosk that the barkeeper specializes in exploiting people's vices. Tosk apologizes to the Ferengi for not having any vices to exploit. Quark is eager to take up this challenge, but O'Brien assures him that Tosk is quite serious. Quark proposes some variety of Holosuite adventure. Tosk replies that he has no need of fantasy adventures, as his life is already the greatest adventure anyone could ask for.

Teleplay by Jill Sherman Donner and Michael Piller
Story by Jill Sherman Donner

Directed by Corey Allen

Regular Cast:
Avery Brooks as Commander Benjamin Sisko
Rene Auberjonois as Odo
Siddig El Fadil as Doctor Bashir
Terry Farrell as Lieutenant Dax
Cirroc Lofton as Jake Sisko
Colm Meaney as Chief O'Brien
Armin Shimerman as Quark
Nana Visitor as Major Kira

Guest Stars:
Gerrit Graham
Scott MacDonald
Kelly Curtis

O'Brien is more than slightly intrigued by this statement, but Tosk cannot explain it any further.

Later, O'Brien discusses their perplexing guest with Sisko. It seems likely that Tosk is running from something, but what, he cannot say. Since Tosk's ship will soon be ready, Sisko feels that their only option will be to speed their guest on his way.

But Tosk is in the hallway outside the weapons area, trying to access the room. A painting on the wall proves, in fact, to be the ever-vigilant Odo, who confronts Tosk over his activities. Rather than answer, Tosk disappears. Odo sets up perimeter force fields, blocking Tosk's way in both directions of the hallway, and finally Tosk reappears and agrees to go along with Odo, promising not to fight.

Confronted by Sisko, Tosk still will not reveal anything about himself, who he's running from, or why he was trying to get access to the weapons. Sisko has no choice but to order Tosk confined to the brig. Perhaps whoever is pursuing him will turn up looking for him. Tosk does not fight, but he is clearly distressed by this turn of events, and he keeps asking to be allowed to "die with honor." When O'Brien questions him about this, Tosk, as usual, has no answers to give.

Soon enough, another ship from the Gamma Quadrant arrives through the wormhole, and sensors indicate that it operates on the same principle as Tosk's vessel. But this ship will not respond to any of Sisko's hails from Deep Space Nine. They do, however, scan the space station. Sisko orders the shields to be raised. The aliens begin to bombard the space station with some unknown form of radiation which reverses the polarity of the shields and leaves Deep Space Nine all but defenseless. Three aliens beam over to the Promenade section, near the brig, and Sisko goes to investigate with Kira and O'Brien in tow. The silent aliens wear red uniforms with boots and round helmets with glowing blue face plates, and they carry weapons shaped, oddly enough, like crossbows. Sisko and his officers draw their phasers. He introduces himself in classic Jim Kirk fashion, but they seem to ignore his words completely. Odo, unarmed, moves forward, only to find himself knocked head over heels by the lead alien.

The intruders then begin to move forward, and Major Kira is the first to fire her phaser at them. But the aliens have some sort of device— a wire attached to their left arms— which absorb the energy of the phaser blasts and somehow dissipate it. The one drawback to this device is that the aliens must block the phaser blasts with an arm movement. A few more phaser blasts, and Sisko scores a direct hit on an alien, who falls to the ground, stunned. A second alien is downed by a shot from O'Brien, but by this time the first one is already getting up again! A security officer fires from an upper level, hitting one of the aliens in the back— but the alien only falls down, gets back up and goes along his way.

Sisko orders an increase in phaser setting— maybe that will slow the intruders down. In a keen burst of insight, Odo guesses that the aliens have come for Tosk. Major Kira points out that they might very well have a legitimate claim to him— but Odo says that he's not about to let anyone take a prisoner out of his brig while he's alive.

O'Brien scores another direct hit, but the aliens keep coming. The phaser increase obviously slows them down more, but not enough to stop them. Kira offers Odo a phaser bet he declines, as he never uses them. Kira nails another alien, but the leader of the intruders aims his weapon at the door to the prison area and lets loose a potent blast that destroys the heavy metal portals. He finds Tosk's prison cell, enclosed with a force field, which seems empty. The alien activates a red beam on his helmet which scans the cell, revealing Tosk, who becomes visible when he realizes that his presence is known. The lead alien speaks to his two companions through a communications device and tells them that he has Tosk, and they beam back to their ship, ending the battle on the Promenade.

The alien removes his helmet; his facial structure is similar to Tosk's but he lacks the scales and the reptilian look; he also has hair, as if he were a mammalian version of his quarry. He addresses Tosk, telling him that he is terribly disappointed. The fight with the humans was entertaining, but to find Tosk a helpless prisoner strikes him as pathetic, and the hunt a waste of time.

Sisko bursts in at this point and overhears these words. He is outraged. Was all of this just part of some alien sporting event? The notion clearly offends him. The alien explains: Tosk are bred for the hunt, to be the perfect quarry, but this one is a disgrace, and, instead of dying honorably, he will be condemned to live out his life on public display.

Sisko is so angry about all this that he refuses to turn Tosk over to the aliens, and threatens to fire on their ship if they give him any more trouble over the matter. The alien is baffled by this response, and even Tosk seems unhappy with the situation. The alien explains that, this poor example notwithstanding, the Tosk are honored by his people. If Sisko's species does not care for their customs, the aliens will be more than happy to make the wormhole out of bounds for future hunts. It was, after all, only a matter of chance that led Tosk, and then them, through it. The alien then beams off the station.

After some consideration, Sisko realizes that he must hand Tosk over to his pursuers. The Prime Directive all but demands it. He can't interfere in their culture no matter how much it might offend him. O'Brien objects, but there's nothing Sisko can do. Major Kira suggests that Tosk could ask for asylum. Sisko agrees that he could give that to their guest, but only if he asks for it.

O'Brien goes to the brig to tell Tosk of the possibility of asylum, but Tosk will not seek it, as it would be even more dishonorable than the dismal fate that awaits him back home. His entire reason for existence is to survive until he dies with honor; now, despite his dishonor, he must continue to play by the same rules. O'Brien leaves, struggling hard to understand his friend's philosophy.

In Quark's bar, the Ferengi strikes up a conversation with the morose Chief O'Brien. Quark's a bit unhappy himself. The new arrivals from the Gamma Quadrant don't seem to be much interested in drinking. O'Brien explains the Hunt, half to Quark and half to himself. Offhandedly, he muses that a Ferengi would probably just change the rules if they didn't suit him. Quark admits that to the Ferengi, rules are always subject to interpretation, but by this point O'Brien has had a brainstorm and has left the bar.

A reluctant Odo prepares to turn Tosk over to his pursuers, and is appalled when the alien places a shackle around Tosk's neck, even when it is explained that it is part of the ritual. O'Brien arrives to escort both aliens to the Transporter. When Odo protests that this is his job, O'Brien lies, claiming that he is acting on Sisko's orders, which prompts Odo to storm off in search of the Commander. The alien hunter is himself unsure about this. His own ship's Transporter will serve just fine. But O'Brien improvises some talk about making up for the earlier misunderstanding, establishing good relationships between cultures, and so on. The alien buys it, and allows O'Brien to lead them away. O'Brien removes his communications badge and leaves it behind.

On the way to the Transporter, O'Brien directs the alien (who of course must lead his captive) through a doorway with a security field, which O'Brien has tampered with. The alien is stunned when he is jolted by a strong energy burst; this isn't enough to keep him down, but a direct punch in the jaw, courtesy of O'Brien, works remarkably well, prompting O'Brien to comment

that he now knows why the alien usually wears a helmet.

As O'Brien leads Tosk back to his ship, the alien manages to broadcast a message to his crew: "The Hunt has resumed." More helmeted aliens begin beaming aboard. One attacks Tosk, but Tosk gets the better of him, and O'Brien leads Tosk into a conduit that will lead to the docking ring, where he removes Tosk's neck shackle.

In Ops, Odo's complaint about O'Brien reveals the Chief's actions to Sisko. Sensors determine their presence in the conduit, and Odo moves to block their passage with a force filed, but Sisko suddenly tells Odo to take his time; there's no reason to hurry. Comprehension crosses Odo's face, and he takes up a position and Ops and stands perfectly still, doing absolutely nothing.

Another alien blocks Tosk's path, but he defeats him and takes his weapon. Three more of them, including their leader, beam directly into their path, but Tosk fires on them with his captured weapon. Finally, they reach the ship. Tosk invites O'Brien to join him in the Hunt, but O'Brien must decline, so Tosk bids him farewell by wishing him a death with honor. After a thoughtful pause, O'Brien responds in kind: "Die with honor, Tosk." And Tosk takes off, to elude his pursuers once more.

An irate Sisko confronts O'Brien and asks him to explain what happened. O'Brien plays innocent, claiming that the security field must have overloaded thanks to all the gear the alien was wearing. When pressed by Sisko, he admits that he did boost the power to the field by about two hundred percent. Sisko gives him a good chewing out, but the basic upshot of the lecture is—don't do it again. O'Brien begins to leave, but pauses and comments on how long it took security to respond. Sisko brushes this off and dismisses O'Brien, but as soon as he is alone, a slight smile sneaks across his lips. After all, what the aliens really wanted was a good Hunt—and now they have one again.

"Q LESS"

In the bar, Julian is explaining a heroic experience he once had to his date of the evening, a lovely young woman. It turns out he's bragging about an exam he took in medical school. O'Brien is sitting at a nearby table and he can't quite believe what he's hearing.

Just then O'Brien and Julian are ordered to Landing Bay 5. A ship is trapped in the landing hold. They manage to get the bulkhead door open and find Dax with a crewman and a passenger they picked up in the wormhole. The passenger is Vash.

Vash has been in the Gamma Quadrant for two years and as she and the others are helped out of the ship, another nearby crewman turns around and we see that he is actually Q.

In Sickbay, Vash is examined and given a clean bill of health. Julian in particular is impressed by Vash, as he is by most any attractive young woman.

When Dax reports to Commander Benjamin Sisko, he wonders openly how Vash could have been in the Gamma Quadrant for two years when the wormhole was only recently discovered. Dax states that Vash is evasive about how she got there, stating that it's a personal matter she does not wish to talk about.

When Vash turns over her belongings for safe keeping, she questions the security arrangements for them as her artifacts are quite rare. These archaeological treasures were all found by her in the Gamma Quadrant. One of these treasures is an orange crystal which glows strangely. One of the personnel says that it looks like Promethean Quartz, but she states that it isn't.

Commander Sisko encounters Vash on the Promenade deck and states that the Daystrom Institute would like to interview her about what she found in the Gamma Quadrant. She's impressed and decides that she would like to return to Earth. Suddenly there's a power drain on the station but the source of

the drain cannot be determined. They are able to compensate but the fact that they don't know the cause is troubling.

O'Brien escorts Vash to her quarters. When she realizes that he had previously served on the Enterprise, she inquires about Jean-Luc Picard and how he's doing. Once alone inside her quarters, Q appears. She's not pleased to see him. She had left Q in the Gamma Quadrant, where he had taken her, and she doesn't care to see him again. Q points out that Vash is persona non grata on several worlds, but that if she stays with him they can go anywhere and do anything. She finds Q an arrogant know-it-all. But when Q points out that he really does know it all, Vash states that the fact that he does really know it all just makes him even more insufferable.

Quark arrives at Vash's quarters to ask about the antiquities she brought aboard and what she plans to do with them. They discuss terms and Vash pretends to come on to Quark, which excites the Ferengi. Quark finally agrees to broker the sale of the items for a twenty-two percent commission.

Shortly thereafter, Julian arrives at Vash's quarters and invites her to dinner. Q plays hide and seek behind Julian as Q is still trying to make up with her, but Vash ignores him.

In the Promenade, Q appears and warns Julian to leave Vash alone and then makes the doctor so sleepy that he returns to his quarters. But in the process O'Brien sees and recognizes Q, exclaiming, "Bloody Hell!" at the sight of him. O'Brien immediately reports the sighting of Q to Commander Sisko. Sisko states that he had a briefing once about Q and the powers that mysterious race possess, but he can't imagine what Q would want aboard Deep Space 9.

Sisko finds Vash and questions her about Q, who is nearby and turns around when he hears his name. He asks Sisko, "Tell me, is Starfleet penalizing you are did you actually request such a dismal command?"

Commander Sisko demands to know why Q is there and tells him to leave the station alone. Q denies being behind the power outages. When Sisko wants to speak to Q in private, Q makes everyone else in the room disappear. When Sisko says to bring them back, Q does, but now Sisko and Q are the two participants in a boxing match that everyone else is cheering on. Sisko won't put up with it and punches Q in the jaw. Q is very surprised.

Aliens begin to arrive at Deep Space 9 for Quark's auction of the archaeological treasures from the Gamma Quadrant. Vash doesn't like the looks of them, but Quark says that it doesn't matter what they look like because they all have money.

There are more power outages, and they're getting more serious. But Sisko no longer believes that Q is behind it. It's not his style. Besides, Q would have taken credit for it. They start trying to trace the source of the power drains.

Odo meets with Quark to discuss the auction as he eavesdropped on Vash and the Ferengi and knows what is going down. Quark claims that everything is on the up and up.

Vash arrives for the auction and Q is still trying to talk Vash into coming back to him as his companion. Q demonstrates to Vash what would have happened if he hadn't been there when she was bitten by a certain insect. Vash finds herself becoming hunched and deformed, but it leaves just as quickly as it began, although she is clearly impressed by what Q showed her.

Q goes to Commander Sisko and warns him to watch out for Vash, that she's not as innocent as she seems.

As the auction is ready to begin, Quark tries to convince Vash to team up with him and go after more artifacts which they can profit by auctioning off. But Vash plans to go back to Earth and retire.

The power drains worsen and the station begins to drift out of position and towards the wormhole. If it enters the wormhole, Deep Space Nine will be ripped apart.

The auction continues as Vash begins to auction off a statue. But she isn't very good at it and so Quark quickly steps in and demonstrates very successfully how it should be done.

A sensor sweep of the station indicates that the power drain is in the central core area.

Q is observing the auction and he decides to announce to everyone there what is happening to the station. Vash accuses Q of causing the station to leave orbit. But the power drain is traced to the glowing, orange crystal being auctioned off. First 600 bars are bid for it.

The station is three minutes from being sucked into the wormhole.

Three thousand bars are bid for the crystal, but just then Sisko arrives and orders that the crystal be immediately beamed off the station. The crystal was actually an egg from which an alien life form was in the process of hatching. When the crystal materializes out in space, the creature emerges from the crystal and flies into the wormhole.

Quark is heart-broken. He hadn't yet been paid for the crystal when it was beamed off the station.

Q advises Vash against going to Earth. "Mind-numbingly dull," he states, pronouncing his verdict on the world. Q says she should go to Tartares 5 where ancient ruins have just been discovered. She decides that she will go there, but without Q.

Teleplay by Robert Hewitt Wolfe
Story by Hannah Louise Shearer

Directed by Paul Lynch

Regular Cast:
Avery Brooks as Commander Benjamin Sisko
Rene Auberjonois as Odo
Siddig El Fadil as Doctor Bashir
Terry Farrell as Lieutenant Dax
Cirroc Lofton as Jake Sisko
Colm Meaney as Chief O'Brien
Armin Shimerman as Quark
Nana Visitor as Major Kira

Guest Stars:
John DeLancie: Q
Jennifer Hetrick: Vash
Van Epperson: Bajoran Clerk
Tom McLeister: Kolos
Laura Cameron: Bajoran Woman

"DAX"

Julian and Dax are sitting at a table on the Promenade, unaware that they are being spied on. The eavesdroppers converse among themselves and it becomes clear that they are after Dax.

Julian walks Dax to her quarters and then leaves. As soon as he goes around a bend in the corridor, several men confront Dax and try to place her under arrest. Julian hears the struggle and he runs back and interferes, but it is to no avail as he is overpowered and Dax is subdued.

When Julian comes to his senses he immediately contacts Commander Sisko, who seals off the station to prevent anyone from leaving. Sisko also discovers that the tractor beam has been disabled and he has it restored to full power.

Dax and her captors are temporarily halted at airlock 5, but one of them over-rides the force field. They board their ship and leave, but the restored tractor beam captures it and pulls it back into the station.

When the airlock door opens to reveal Dax and her captors, Odo orders them out at gun point, stating, "Slowly. Extremities where I can see them." They free Dax from her captors.

The leader of the captors is from Klystron 4 and he announces that Dax is guilty of treason and the murder of his father. The crime took place thirty years before when the Trill was in the form of Curzon Dax. Curzon Dax is accused of betraying Klystron 4 to the rebels and causing the death of a famous military commander.

Commander Sisko goes to Jadzia Dax in her quarters to talk with her about all this, but she is unwilling to discuss it. This infuriates Sisko as he considers her a friend and Curzon Dax was his mentor. Dax apologies but says that she cannot talk about it.

When the representative from Klystron 4 makes his official request to extradite Jadzia Dax, Sisko points out that Deep Space Nine is Bajoran, and Klystron has no extradition treaty with Bajor. Klystron knew this, which was why they tried to kidnap Dax and circumvent official channels. But according to regulations, an extradition hearing will be held on Deep Space Nine to determine whether the claims made by Klystron have any merit.

Odo goes to Quark and informs the Ferengi that they'll have to use his bar for the extradition hearing. Quark's does not like this because it will severely disrupt his business.

Commander Sisko meets with Odo and suggests that Odo travel to Klystron 4 to investigate the charges and determine whether there is any truth to support the accusations since Dax won't cooperate in helping them defend her.

The extradition hearing begins after the official Federation arbiter arrives. She makes it clear that she doesn't want a long, drawn out proceeding and orders them all to dispense with any extraneous verbiage. The reason that this charge is only coming out now is that the circumstantial evidence against Curzon Dax was in military files which were sealed until just recently.

Sisko states that he wants to see proof that this is the same Dax as the one accused of these crimes. During a recess, Sisko suggests using the computer library to investigate the crime.

Teleplay by D.C. Fontana and Peter Allan Fields
Story by Peter Allan Fields

Regular Cast:
Avery Brooks as Commander Benjamin Sisko
Rene Auberjonois as Odo
Siddig El Fadil as Doctor Bashir
Terry Farrell as Lieutenant Dax
Cirroc Lofton as Jake Sisko
Colm Meaney as Chief O'Brien
Armin Shimerman as Quark
Nana Visitor as Major Kira

Guest Stars:
Gregory Itzin
Anne Haney
Richard Lineback
Fionnula

They search for legal decisions regarding Trills.

A subspace message from Odo reveals that Curzon Dax and the General were the best of friends, and that the murder of the General inspired his troops to retaliate against the rebels and defeat them, thereby winning the war for Klystron 4.

Odo visits the General's widow who states flatly that Curzon Dax did not kill her husband, and says that the evidence against Dax is all circumstantial. She becomes upset when she learns that Curzon died and that Dax is in a new host body.

At the extradition hearing back on Deep Space Nine, another Trill has been brought in to testify. He explains what a Trill is. It's a blending of symbiont and host, not the domination of one over the other.

Dr. Bashir testifies that the two Daxes have different brainwave patterns. But Julian admits there is no evidence of any change in the symbiont's brainwave patterns between hosts.

Commander Sisko testifies and is cross examined by Major Kira. Sisko states that Curzon Dax was different from Jadzia Dax. Their personalities were different.

Jadzia Dax is slated to take the stand in the hearing after the recess, but she makes it clear that she will do so only with great reluctance.

Back on Klystron 4, Odo discovers that Curzon Dax and the General's wife had been having an affair thirty years before. Odo confronts the General's widow and she admits it. She states that she doesn't mourn her husband because she knows what he was really like. He wasn't the hero the world believes he was. She agrees to go to Deep Space Nine and tell the truth about what happened that day thirty years ago.

Odo reports to Sisko about what he's discovered. Ben Sisko goes to Jadzia Dax and reveals that he knows about the affair with the General's wife. But Dax still doesn't want to talk about it. She feels the shame of Curzon's indiscretion.

At the hearing, Jadzia explains how she strived to be chosen as a host body and that all of the degrees she has were obtained before she merged with Dax.

The General's widow, Anina Tondro, arrives and reveals that Curzon Dax was in her bed with her when the transmission in question was sent to the rebels. The General sent that transmission as he had sold out to the rebels and the rebels in turn killed him. Anina's son is very upset by this turn of events as he has discovered that his father was not the hero he grew up believing him to be. Anina thanks Dax for trying to protect her as the General is the one who committed treason.

Dax later explains to Sisko that she felt she could not reveal what she knew without betraying Curzon, even though he's now dead. Sisko realizes that Trills are more complex than even he believed.

"THE PASSENGER"

Major Kira is in the shuttle Rio Grande with Dr. Bashir, who recently saved a woman's life and he's discussing the experience with her. The shuttle picks up a distress signal on their long range sensors. The Rio Grande responds.

Julian and Major Kira beam over to the disabled ship and discover that it is on fire. A prisoner is being transported and the injured guard says not to release him because the prisoner is dangerous. But Dr. Bashir doesn't feel that he can just leave the man to die so he opens the cell door and enters, finding the prisoner injured on the floor. But as Julian leans over him the prisoner grabs the doctor by the throat. Then the prisoner dies.

Back on Deep Space Nine, Dr. Bashir revives the guard they rescued from the disabled transport vessel. She demands to see the dead prisoner's body as she wants to be certain that it's the same body and that he's really dead. Dr. Bashir confirms that the body is that of Vantakar, the prisoner, and that he's definitely deceased.

The police officer has tracked Vantakar for twenty years and she explains that the man was a scientist who killed to prolong his own life.

In Quark's place, Odo and Quark argue over whether Dax is attracted to the Ferengi. Odo doesn't think it's possible but Quark states that it's good to want things you can't have.

A deridium shipment is due at the station and Odo, the chief of security, is watching Quark carefully to insure that the Ferengi has no designs on stealing the valuable cargo. The deridium is for a dying race which needs the element to survive.

A Starfleet security officer named Primmin arrives and he quickly gets on Odo's bad side by questioning the security arrangements for the deridium. The Starfleet security man reports to Sisko. When the man questions Odo's effectiveness, Sisko defends Odo strongly and tells the man to work with him.

The Starfleet officer, Primmin, apologies to Odo and they go over security together as they've discovered a plot to steal the shipment. When they check the computer they discover that its active memory has been purged.

The police officer states that the dead prisoner once did the same thing and she believes that he is somehow still alive and on the station. Sisko states that he just thinks that it was done by an accomplice and does believe that the threat to the deridium is very real.

Odo insists that Commander Sisko give him clear jurisdiction in the security arrangements but Sisko, while granting Odo jurisdiction, also wants him to get along with Primmin.

Jadzia Dax has swept the shuttle Rio Grande with sensors and finds that someone tried to break into it. They were unsuccessful but she believes they were after a small disk she'd already found and which has a map of a humanoid brain on it.

After hours, Quark is searching in his bar for any lost items which he can keep. He is then contacted by the killer, Vantakar, much to his amazement. The man is disguised by a cloak. Quark thought the man was dead. The killer wants the mercenaries that he had previously ordered Quark to hire. Quark says they'll be ready, and then the man mysteriously slips away without revealing anything more.

Dr. Bashir summons the police woman and shows her that his scan confirms the identity of the dead body as that of the criminal, Vantakar.

Later, Jadzia Dax tells Julian that the file disk she found concerns the storage of neural energy patterns, which could mean surviving after death. Dax suggests that the entity could be sharing someone's brain without their even knowing it. They believe that the police woman is the most likely suspect.

The police woman confronts Odo over the fact that she's been restricted from the station's security files. Odo explains that it's part of his security arrangement as only a small number of people now have access to that information.

Vantakar's henchmen are ready and waiting and they tell Quark that they want to get paid in advance. The police officer discovers them and although she cannot hear everything being said she tries to spy on them from a catwalk above them. But she falls and lands right next to the mercenaries, knocking herself unconscious.

In Sickbay she says that Vantakar pushed her. Quark states that he saw her fall from the balcony but didn't see anyone else there. Odo goes to investigate the scene.

Dax is in the stasis room examining Vantakar's body and believes that she has discovered how he transferred his consciousness through something under his fingernails.

Odo talks to Major Kira and discovers that Primmin is missing. Is there any connection? Could Vantakar be hiding in Primmin's body?

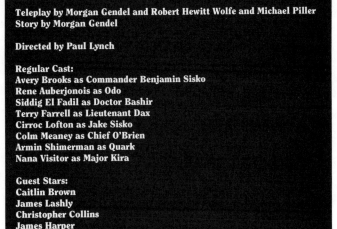

Teleplay by Morgan Gendel and Robert Hewitt Wolfe and Michael Piller
Story by Morgan Gendel

Directed by Paul Lynch

Regular Cast:
Avery Brooks as Commander Benjamin Sisko
Rene Auberjonois as Odo
Siddig El Fadil as Doctor Bashir
Terry Farrell as Lieutenant Dax
Cirroc Lofton as Jake Sisko
Colm Meaney as Chief O'Brien
Armin Shimerman as Quark
Nana Visitor as Major Kira

Guest Stars:
Caitlin Brown
James Lashly
Christopher Collins
James Harper

Quark and the mercenaries enter the runabout Rio Grande and discover that Julian Bashir is there waiting for them. He is Vantakar, and has been in Dr. Bashir's body since grabbing him aboard the stricken spacecraft.

Dax searches for Julian but can only find his con badge. The con badge's are supposed to be always kept with a person as they enable the station computer to locate them no matter where they are.

Primmin has found a subspace shunt which would have shut down the station's power for an hour had it detonated, thereby enabling the easy theft of the diridium while all of the station's defenses were immobilized.

The shuttle containing the diridium arrives but before it can dock with Deep Space Nine, the shuttle Rio Grande goes out to intercept it.

The mercenaries beam over to the transport shuttle and hijack it. Then Julian boards it as well. When the transport shuttle is seized with a tractor beam, Vantakar becomes angry as this wasn't supposed to happen. He has the shuttle engage full power to counteract the tractor beam temporarily.

Sisko contacts Julian and orders him to surrender. Julian states that he'll kill himself if they don't release the tractor beam. Dax thinks she can develop an impulse which will disrupt Vantakar's control over Julian.

Vantakar tells them to release the shuttle now. Dax sends the pulse and Julian regains enough senses to turn off the shuttle's screens before Vantakar takes over his body again. Julian is beamed over to the station and they use a Transporter beam to remove Vantakar's consciousness and imprison it in a small device. Julian is now completely himself again. Julian awakens with a bad headache and doesn't remember any of it.

The police officer destroys the device containing Vantakar's consciousness, thereby executing the prisoner once and for all.

"MOVE ALONG HOME"

Commander Sisko is preparing to meet an alien delegation which is arriving from the Gamma Quadrant. This will be the Federation's first contact with the beings who call themselves the Waddi. Ben talks with his son, Jake, and discovers that the boy has become interested in girls, thanks to Nog, Quark's nephew.

Sisko is notified that the Waddi will be arriving at docking bay four. The senior staff, which includes Dax, Dr. Bashir and Major Kira are all there waiting to greet the alien delegation. Julian is flustered because he couldn't find his dress uniform. Sisko arrives and is nervous, wanting to make the best first impression he can on the aliens.

When the Waddi emerge from the docking bay, Fallow, the leader of the delegation, cuts Sisko's greetings short and asks where the games are that he's heard of at Quark's place. As the Waddi walk away towards the Promenade area after having all but ignored Sisko and his senior staff, the commander remarks, "First contact is not what it used to be."

At Quark's place, the Ferengi inquires of Sisko whether the aliens have any money. Sisko doesn't know and tries to explain that this isn't the point. This is first contact with a new species.

Quark talks to Fallow, the leader of the Waddi delegation, who states that his people like games. Quark directs the Waddi to the roulette wheel, but Quark wants to see a wager. He rejects a supposedly "priceless" wine, observing, "One man's priceless is another man's worthless."

Then Fallow dumps out a small sack of gems over which Quark becomes excited. "Get these folks some drinks," he orders.

Six hours later, the Waddi are still playing roulette and Sisko is very bored. He decides to turn in for the night and tells Quark to keep the visitors happy.

Teleplay by Frederick Rappaport and Lisa Rich & Jeanne Carrigan-Fauci
Story by Michael Piller

Directed by David Carson

Regular Cast:
Avery Brooks as Commander Benjamin Sisko
Rene Auberjonois as Odo
Siddig El Fadil as Doctor Bashir
Terry Farrell as Lieutenant Dax
Cirroc Lofton as Jake Sisko
Colm Meaney as Chief O'Brien
Armin Shimerman as Quark
Nana Visitor as Major Kira

Guest Stars:
Clara Bryant: Chandra
Joel Brooks
James Lashly

But Quark is unhappy that the Waddi keep winning at roulette, so he rigs the wheel to make them lose.

Jake comes home late and Ben Sisko is annoyed that his son spends so much time with Nog. He says he wants to have a talk with Jake the next morning before the boy goes to school.

Fallow catches Quark cheating on the roulette wheel and to make up for it, the Ferengi tries to offer the Waddi a free visit to the holo-suite, which offers a variety of erotic delights. "Do you have sex on your world?" Quark wonders.

Instead, Fallow demonstrates a different game which he had brought with him, and which materializes before Quark's eyes.

When Commander Sisko awakens, he finds himself lying on a floor which isn't in his quarters. He tries using his con badge to contact the station but he can't connect with security or with the Deep Space Nine computer. At first he thinks he must be on a holo-deck and orders the program to end, but nothing happens. When he begins to explore his surroundings, he opens a door and sees Fallow who exclaims, "Move along home!" before disappearing behind the door.

When Ben Sisko hears shouting, he finds Julian who was yelling because he thought he was dreaming and was trying to wake himself up. Dr. Bashir is glad to find out he wasn't dreaming. Major Kira and Dax have also been attracted by the shouting and they team up to find out what's going on.

Major Kira is annoyed by all this. But they do find that their con badges still work among themselves so that they can remain in touch with one another.

On Deep Space Nine, morning has arrived and Jake goes to Odo and asks if he knows where Commander Sisko. Odo reassures the boy and tells him to go to school while he finds the commander. When Odo discovers that Sisko is indeed off the station without a trace, he becomes annoyed. Going to the main security station he tells them to search for the entire senior staff who are all apparently missing.

Fallow tells Quark that he must learn the rules of the game as they play. Quark rolls the dice and is told that his pieces will meet the Chandra. Fallow programs the game.

Meanwhile, Sisko and the others encounter a child in a room. They were attracted to that room by her reciting of a rhyme. When they enter and see her, the door closes behind them, blocking their retreat. They must go forward.

Major Kira moves forward but encounters a force field. But they can see that the child has no trouble moving through the field. They figure out that they must both follow her steps on certain squares on the floor as well as recite her rhyme to move through the force field.

Quark wins that level of the game and Fallow hands him gems. Now he must choose a new path for his players. Quark is beginning to like this game and suggests adding it to his establishment.

When Odo goes to Quark and says that four staff members are missing. Quark suddenly realizes that Fallow told him he has four pieces in the game.

"Double their peril—double your winnings," Fallow states. Odo picks up on this and Quark nervously chooses the safer path.

Inside the maze, they figure out that this is some sort of game. They enter another area where the Waddi are having a party in a smoke-filled room. The four start becoming overcome by the smoke until Julian notices that none of the Waddi are affected and all of them are holding drinking glasses. He grabs one and drinks and discovers that it is the antidote to the smoke and gives it to the others so that they quickly recover. The Waddi abruptly disappear from the room.

On the game board, the four pieces advance.

Odo is trying to scan the Waddi vessel, but is unsuccessful. Odo has himself beamed over to the Waddi vessel, but upon opening the door to a room he finds himself beamed back to Quark's place. Odo demands that the game be stopped. "End the game, lose all your players," Fallow states.

Quark rolls the dice, but Fallow pronounces it an unfortunate roll.

In the maze they see triangular light formations coming towards them down a corridor, lights which group into a single globe of energy and seemingly attack Julian and make the doctor disappear.

In Quark's place, Fallow knocks over a game piece.

Quark says to take the short route although Odo argues against it, but Quark explains they could go all the way home on one move. "Trust a gambler," Quark promises. He has Odo blow on the dice for luck.

Fallow says that Quark must sacrifice one so that two may live. Quark won't do it and starts breaking down, begging them not to make him do this and in return he'll never cheat again. Fallow agrees that Quark doesn't have to sacrifice one—the game will make the choice.

In the maze they hear Julian calling and so they search for him in a cavern-like room where they encounter a rockfall which injures Dax. The person they think is Julian turns out to be Fallow who states, "Move along home!"

Sisko and Kira help Dax and find themselves on a ledge overlooking an abyss. Dax says to leave her behind. Kira and Sisko could make the jump to another ledge, but not with Dax. Dax insists they go on without her, but they refuse.

Finally the cave begins to crumble and all three fall into the abyss and then abruptly appear in Quark's place.

Fallow tells Quark, "I'm afraid all your players were lost."

"You mean we were never in any real danger?" Kira asks.

"It's only a game," Fallow replies, and then says that it's time to move along home.

Sisko is furious over the way they were used, but Odo explains that this was all Quark's fault because he was caught cheating. The Waddi leave and say that perhaps some day they could have a rematch.

Quark decides that he likes the game after all and hurries after the Waddi to discuss including it in Quark's place.

"THE NAGUS"

A cloaked and hooded Ferengi arrives on Deep Space Nine with his retainers.

Jake is in his room getting ready for something when his father, Ben, surprises the boy and says that he wants to take him down to a festival on the planet Bajor. But Jake would rather stay on the station with his friend, Nog.

Quark abuses his brother, Rom, for returning a lost currency pouch to its owner. As punishment, Quark orders Rom to polish every rail in the bar. Rom then orders his son, Nog, to perform the punishment in retaliation for an imagined infraction.

The Grand Nagus, Zek, arrives and wants to use Quark's holo-suite. Quark is concerned that the programs could be too energetic for Zek but the Nagus wants to try all five of Quark's personal favorites.

In the school aboard the station, Miles O'Brien is substituting for Keiko. He asks Nog about the essay on ethics he was supposed to write for an assignment. Nog doesn't have it, claiming that his notepad was stolen by Vulcans—because they don't have ethics. His classmates laugh at him. But Nog gets Jake to reluctantly back up his story.

In Quark's place, he's concerned about the Nagus because he believes that Zek is there to buy the place—at a fraction of its worth.

Ben talks to O'Brien about the class and Miles admits that he's concerned about Jake and Nog. O'Brien doesn't think that Nog is a good influence. But Ben says that he trusts his son.

At Quark's place they're eating live grubs and the Nagus likes them. Zek mentions running into Quark's cousin, who just got out of prison after serving time for a crime that Quark was involved with.

Zek is dismayed to learn that Nog attends a school run by humans. Rom then immediately orders Nog to stay away from school. Then the Nagus announces that he wants to use Quark's bar to host a conference the next day.

Major Kira reports to Commander Sisko that the third Ferengi ship in twenty four hours has arrived at the station.

At Quark's place the conference begins when the Nagus makes his entrance. Jake finds Nog, who states that he doesn't belong in the school, and yet the young Ferengi seems very angry over the turn of events.

The Nagus says that it's harder to find business opportunities in the Alpha Quadrant because their reputation precedes them. But the Gamma Quadrant is wide open and the Ferengi are unknown there. The Nagus states that he is too old to spearhead this himself and so chooses his successor—Quark. The conference breaks up as the other Ferengi express outrage over the choice.

Meanwhile, Jake is depressed. He tells Ben that Nog has been pulled out of school. Ben explains that human values and Ferengi values are very different.

Quark is warned that those who are jealous might harm Quark in order to take his place. Quark goes to Zek because he feels that he's been threatened. "When in doubt, be ruthless," Zek states. Then Zek dies.

Teleplay by Ira Steven Behr
Story by David Livingston

Directed by David Livingston

Regular Cast:
Avery Brooks as Commander Benjamin Sisko
Rene Auberjonois as Odo
Siddig El Fadil as Doctor Bashir
Terry Farrell as Lieutenant Dax
Cirroc Lofton as Jake Sisko
Colm Meaney as Chief O'Brien
Armin Shimerman as Quark
Nana Visitor as Major Kira

Guest Stars:
Wallace Shawn: Zek
Max Grodenchik
Lou Wagner
Tiny Ron
Barry Gordon
Lee Arenberg
Aron Eisenberg

Now Quark feels really alone and he wants his brother, Rom, to be his bodyguard as he's the only one he can trust any more. Odo is suspicious about Zek's death and wants Dr. Bashir to examine the body, but Zek's son explains that it has already been vacuum desiccated and partitioned to sell. After all, Zek was very famous.

At Zek's funeral, Quark barely avoids an assassination attempt. He bends down to pick up a dropped coin and a flying bomb just misses him.

Odo and Sisko go to talk to Quark, who was uninjured by the flying bomb. They want to know who would gain by Quark's death. They discover that Zek's servant was not at the funeral where the assassination attempt occurred, which is odd since the servant was extremely loyal to the Nagus.

Meanwhile, Jake and Nog are meeting to do something in secret which the boy doesn't feel he can reveal to his father. Quark is meeting with other

Ferengi whom he questions about their loyalty. He also makes a lucrative deal. After Quark leaves, Rom plots his brother's death.

Dax comes to see Sisko and finds that Jake is late for dinner. Dax says that she understands what Ben is going through because she's been a mother three times and a father twice. Dax says that Ben should find Jake and bring him home. He goes to look for Jake and the computer states that the boy is in cargo bay 14. Ben secretly observes the two boys and discovers that Jake is there tutoring Nog and decides not to disturb them.

Quark is preparing to travel to the wormhole to complete negotiations on a planet being opened there for trade. Rom and Zek's son are going to be accompanying Quark. Quark wants to bring a girl but he is talked out of it. Meanwhile, Odo is following Zek's servant.

In the docking bay, Quark enters an airlock and suddenly finds himself sealed in there alone. Quark begs his brother for help. Just as Rom is about to blast Quark out of the airlock into the vacuum of space, Zek appears, alive and well. Odo arrives at the same time along with Zek and Quark is released.

Zek never died but was just in a special self-induced trance. It was all a way for Zek to test his son as to whether he was ready for leadership. But Zek says that his son failed miserably. He should have let Quark be Nagus while using the bar to gather information as information is power.

Zek is still the Nagus and plans to leave for the Gamma Quadrant. He tells Quark that the bar is very profitable and says that one day he'll come back and buy it from him.

Quark is impressed with Rom for trying to kill him. "I didn't think you had the lobes!" Quark exclaims. He rewards Rom by giving him a title. It's meaningless, but it's a title.

Ben sees Jake with Nog and he embraces his son, saying that it's all right with him if he spends time with Nog.

"VORTEX"

Odo enters Quark's place. To Quark's chagrin, the security chief has his usual, which is nothing. Odo quizzes Quark about a Miradorn ship which just arrived at the station. He is suspicious and he rightly assumes that if there's anyone who would know anything about what the Miradorn want, it would be Quark. But Quark claims ignorance, stating that he avoids the Miradorn because they are so notoriously bad tempered.

Sitting nearby is Crodon, who is someone the Vulcans rescued from a damaged ship they found in the Gamma Quadrant. Quark says that he's spoken to Crodon in passing but doesn't know anything about him.

Two Miradorn men enter the bar and nod to Quark as though in recognition. This arouses Odo's suspicions all over again. Quark becomes angry, stating that of course they would acknowledge him since he's the bar tender. Quark has had enough of Odo's accusations and storms off.

Taking Rom aside, Quark has him prepare a tray with a bottle of wine to take into the back to some special guests—the Miradorn. Odo cannot help but notice this. He apparently has better hearing than Quark would be comfortable knowing about.

In a back room, the Miradorn meet with Quark as Rom comes in with the tray of glasses and the bottle of wine. The Miradorn have a golden egg the size of a man's hand and they want one thousand bars of gold pressed latinum for it. Quark looks at it admiringly, acknowledging its undeniable beauty and his avarice is undisguised. But Quark sadly admits that the buyer he had lined up for the bauble has backed out due to a question over whether the item was acquired legitimately. It has become known that something very similar was stolen in a raid on a vessel just two light years from the station. Quark suggests that if the Miradorn could produce a bill of sale.

The Miradorn become furious, stating that Quark expressed no concern about how they got it before and they threaten the Ferengi, stating that they need him to find another buyer quickly or else!

Suddenly Crodon, the stranger seen in the bar, bursts in, waving a gun and telling everyone not to move and they won't get hurt. It's obviously a robbery attempt. One of the Miradorn attacks Crodon and the tray of glasses is knocked to the floor where one smashes. The smashed glass begins to reform and become Odo.

One of the Miradorn then tries to kill Crodon and he shoots the alien in self-defense, whereupon Odo steps in, disarming the man and preventing further mayhem. But the Miradorn who was shot is dead. The two Miradorn were brothers and with his twin dead the other wants vengeance. When one twin Miradorn is killed, the other suffers.

Odo arrests Crodon and everyone else on the scene and places them in custody until they can be interrogated. Quark is furious and turns on Rom exclaiming, "Five glasses for four people!" as the extra glass should have been noticed. Quark is obviously unhappy about Odo's timely (or was it untimely?) arrival.

The Miradorn appeal to Sisko, demanding that he be allowed to kill Crodon for killing his brother. But Sisko says that this is not the way they do things. The prisoner will stand trial and he orders the Miradorn out of his office.

Since Odo had arrested everyone at the scene of the crime, including Quark, he questions the Ferengi about certain oddities. Quark points out that he was the one who expressed concern over whether the object was stolen, which Odo states is exactly what makes him suspicious. Rom expresses outrage for Odo to be implying that Quark may have been behind the robbery attempt. Quark calls his brother a fool because if the Miradorn come to that conclusion then Quark's life would be valueless. Odo dismisses the Ferengi but it's clear he believes they were involved in the robbery attempt.

Commander Sisko tries to interrogate Crodon, but the prisoner seems bored and uninterested in what happens to him. Odo is observing the questioning and in passing Crodon remarks how much better a thief he would be if he were a changeling like the security chief. Odo is very interested to hear Crodon use that term and wants to know if Crodon has ever met any other changelings. Crodon implies that he has but becomes evasive about what he knows.

Sisko and his senior staff discuss the situation with Crodon. Since he was found in the Gamma Quadrant, he may well be a criminal who is also wanted on his homeworld, wherever that might be. Sisko decides that he wants to find out what planet Crodon came from. And he also wants Odo to make sure that the prisoner is carefully guarded as the Miradorn clearly want him killed.

Odo goes to Quark and questions him about how well he knew Crodon. The Ferengi denies knowing him at all, but Odo states that he knows that Quark was inquiring about the availability of a shuttle capable of going through the wormhole. Crodon would need to return to his world, possibly after completing a little job for Quark. Quark denies this even though Odo has also found people who have seen the Ferengi in long discussions with Crodon on several occasions. Quark denies it and is very upset that anyone might think he was behind the robbery attempt which cost the Miradorn his life. Such reckless speculation could cost Quark his own life.

When the Miradorn demands to have the prisoner again, Odo threatens to arrest the Miradorn if he doesn't back off. Odo then goes to Crodon, who remarks that he and Odo have much in common as they are each one of a kind there on the station. Crodon says that changelings lived on his world long ago and he baits Odo by stating that he knows where a colony of changelings live in the vortex in the Gamma Quadrant. Then he shows Odo proof—a medallion which when opened can change its shape. Odo is fascinated and Crodon freely gives the medallion to him.

Ben Sisko and Jadzia Dax take the shuttle Rio Grande through the wormhole to the planet they believe Crodon came from in the Gamma Quadrant.

Written by Sam Rolfe

Directed by Winrich Kolbe

Regular Cast:
Avery Brooks as Commander Benjamin Sisko
Rene Auberjonois as Odo
Siddig El Fadil as Doctor Bashir
Terry Farrell as Lieutenant Dax
Cirroc Lofton as Jake Sisko
Colm Meaney as Chief O'Brien
Armin Shimerman as Quark
Nana Visitor as Major Kira

Guest stars:
Cliff DeYoung: Crodon
Randy Oglesby
Max Grodenchik
Kathleen Garrett
Leslie Engelberg
Gordon Clapp

Upon arriving in orbit around the planet Rakar, they send a message. They are ignored until they reveal that they have Crodon in their custody and inquire as to whether he is wanted on that world. One of the Rakarians comes on the viewscreen and angrily demands that Crodon be turned over to them immediately. When Sisko explains that he is back on a space station being held for trial, the alien states that Crodon has already been tried in absentia for his crimes and they want him returned. Sisko reluctantly agrees and says that a shuttle like this one will bring Crodon to Rakar in fifty-two hours.

On Deep Space Nine, Dr. Bashir is examining the strange medallion. He says that in some ways it is much like Odo, and although inanimate might be considered a distant cousin. It is the first time that Odo has encountered anything which is like himself.

Odo goes back to Crodon's cell and wants to know where the stone came from. At first Crodon won't answer, and then says that he found it on an asteroid he once hid on inside the Vortex where he found a colony of changelings. He says that he'll take Odo there if the security chief will get him out. Odo seems tempted but it would clearly put him at odds with his duty.

Commander Sisko returns from Rakar and informs Odo that the security chief is to return the prisoner to Crodon's home world of Rakar. But they have to try to leave without the Miradorn detecting them as the aliens are scanning every departing ship to see if Crodon is aboard. The ship the Miradorn have is much faster and more powerful than the shuttle Odo would be using.

Odo puts Crodon aboard a shuttle and he uses a departing freighter to shield them from the Miradorn ship and thereby enter the wormhole undetected and successfully mask their departure.

Aboard the shuttle, Crodon asks Odo how he can stand living where he doesn't belong? Crodon claims that the government of Rakar sent men who burst into his home and murdered both his wives without ever telling him what crime he had committed. On Rakar they punish someone by killing their family. But Crodon managed to slay the security officers who killed his family and then escaped. Odo expresses doubt as to whether Crodon is telling the truth.

The Miradorn storms into Quark's place and demands to know where Crodon is as their scanners can no longer detect him aboard the station. The Miradorn still have suspicions about the Ferengi and Quark hastily agrees to help, using an illegal security chip to break into the computer. Quark finds a log entry from Odo's shuttle which reveals the truth. The Miradorn says that if Quark is lying, he'll come back and kill him.

The Miradorn vessel leaves and even though Commander Sisko attempts to delay its departure using protocol, it ignores him and enters the wormhole.

As the shuttle Rio Grande nears the vortex, Crodon remarks that going through the vortex would be quicker.

Suddenly the Miradorn ship attacks the shuttle. They are hailed and the Miradorn demands that Odo turn over Crodon to him. Odo refuses. The Miradorn ship opens fire again and Crodon states that he can save them by piloting the shuttle into the vortex. Odo reluctantly agrees.

Once inside the Vortex the shuttle still isn't able to evade the Miradorn ship and so Crodon takes it down to an asteroid to avoid detection. "So, shapeshifter, I guess I'll get to take you home after all."

On the asteroid they exit the shuttle and enter a cave. Crodon leads Odo towards a certain chamber, but Odo demands to know if Crodon has been telling him the truth. Crodon admits that he wasn't, that he bought the medallion from a trader. But he does have something hidden in the cavern ahead of them. They come upon a stasis chamber which contains Crodon's daughter. This is the real reason he wanted to return through the wormhole.

Using the medallion which can shape itself into the form of any key, he opens the stasis chamber and Crodon's daughter awakens. She hugs her father and Odo realizes that at least some of what Crodon told him was the truth—the part about having a family, and presumably what happened to his wives as well. Crodon asks Odo to take care of his daughter for him and the security chief agrees to take her someplace safe.

When the Miradorn track them to the asteroid and attack again, the three run for the shuttle. Odo is knocked out by a falling rock, and after hesitating for a moment, Crodon picks up the unconscious Odo and carries him to the shuttlecraft. They take off again and when Odo awakens, Crodon remarks that the security chief is heavier than he looks. Odo is surprised that Crodon didn't just leave him behind. This reveals more about Crodon's character than Odo had believed possible.

Crodon had warned Odo about pockets of explosive fields in the vortex which they must avoid as the blasts from the Miradorn ship could detonate one and destroy them. Odo says that they have to enter one of those fields and in so doing they lure the Miradorn in after them.

The Miradorn orders the shuttle to surrender but when it doesn't, Odo waits until they detect the Miradorn preparing to fire, and then the shuttle flees the explosive field. They just manage to get out as the Miradorn fires, blowing its own vessel up from the volatile reaction of the explosive field.

Crodon again asks Odo to take care of his daughter. But before he can answer they are hailed by a Vulcan ship. Odo states that he has picked up two survivors from a wreck and Odo asks the Vulcan if she will take his two passengers back with her to her home planet. The Vulcan agrees. Odo tells Crodon that he'll just state that his prisoner was killed by the Miradorn on the asteroid.

Crodon and his daughter are beamed aboard the Vulcan ship and Odo returns through the wormhole. But the security chief wonders where his home and his people really are, and if he'll ever find them.

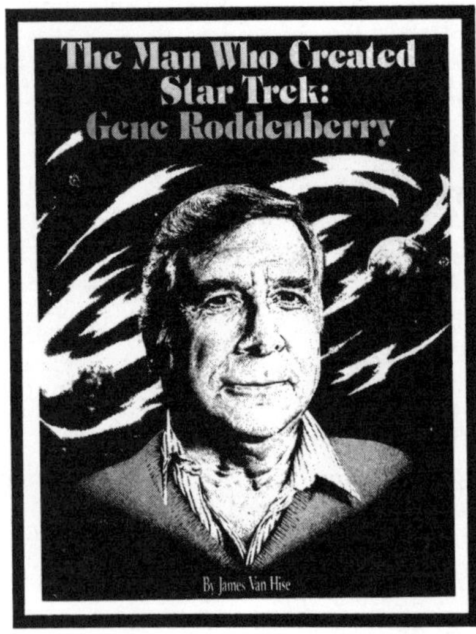

THE MAN WHO CREATED STAR TREK: GENE RODDENBERRY

James Van Hise

The complete life story of the man who created STAR TREK, reveals the man and his work.

$14.95 in stores ONLY $12.95 to Couch Potato Catalog Customers
160 Pages
ISBN # 1-55698-318-2

TWENTY-FIFTH ANNIVERSARY TREK TRIBUTE

James Van Hise

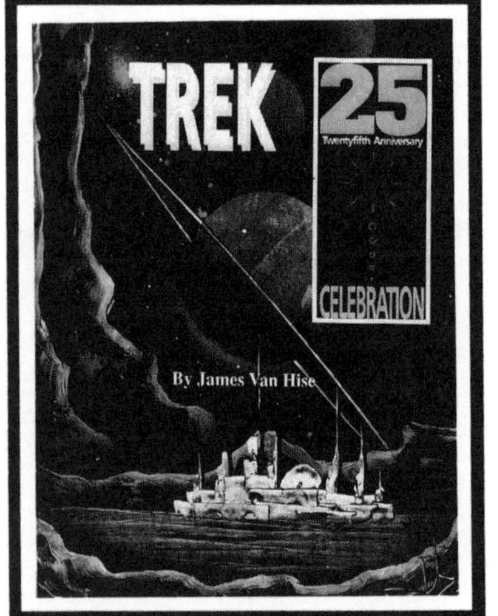

Taking a close up look at the amazing Star Trek stroy, this book traces the history of the show that has become an enduring legend. James Van Hise chronicles the series from 1966 to its cancellation in 1969, through the years when only the fans kept it alive, and on to its unprecedented revival. He offers a look at its latter-day blossoming into an animated series, a sequence of five movies (with a sixth in preparation) that has grossed over $700 million, and the offshoot "The Next Generation" TV series.

The author gives readers a tour of the memorials at the Smithsonian and the Movieland Wax Museums, lets them witness Leonard Nimoy get his star on the Hollywood Walk Of Fame in 1985, and takes them behind the scenes of the motion-picture series and TV's "The Next Generation." The concluding section examines the future of Star Trek beyond its 25th Anniversary.

$14.95.....196 Pages
ISBN # 1-55698-290-9

THE TREK FAN'S HANDBOOK

Written by James Van Hise

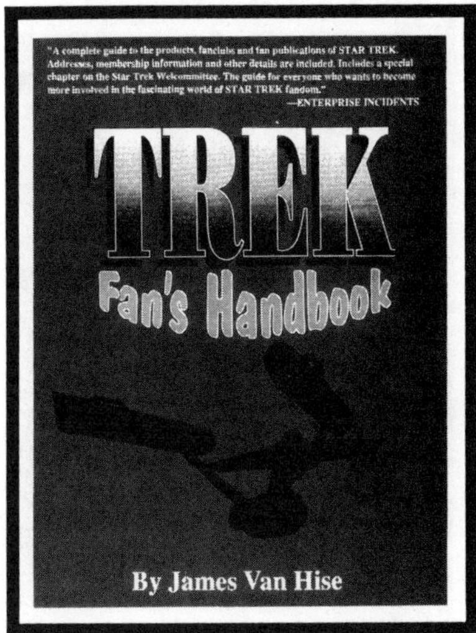

STAR TREK inspired its millions of loyal fans to put pen to paper, in order to discuss the various themes and issues being raised by the show's scripts, explore the characters in minute detail and ponder where both STAR TREK and humanity are headed in the future. THE TREK FAN'S HANDBOOK offers a guide on who to write to, what products are available, information on the various STAR TREK fanclubs, addresses, membership information nad details on the fanzines they publish.

THE TREK FAN'S HANDBOOK allows the reader to tap into the basic backbone of what has allowed STAR TREK to thrive over the past quarter century.

$9.95.....109 Pages
ISBN # 1-55698-271-2

TREK: THE NEXT GENERATION

James Van Hise

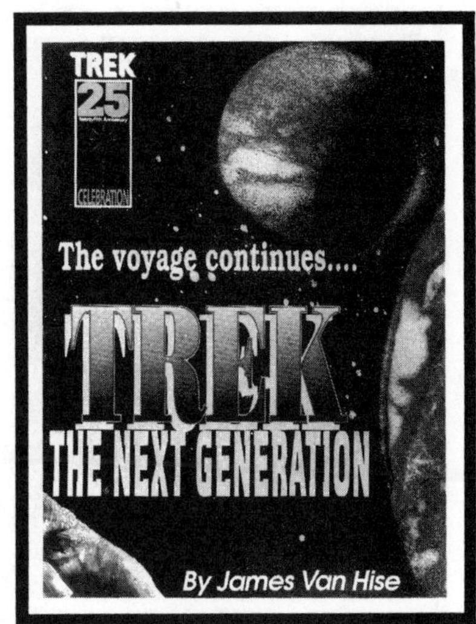

They said it would not last, and after its cancellation in 1969, it looked as if it wouldn't. But the fans refused to let it die and now *Star Trek* is thriving as never before. The *Next Generation* television series continues the adventure. This book reveals the complete story behind the new series, the development of each major character, presents a complete episode guide, and gives plans for the future.

$14.95.....164 Pages
ISBN # 1-55698-305-0

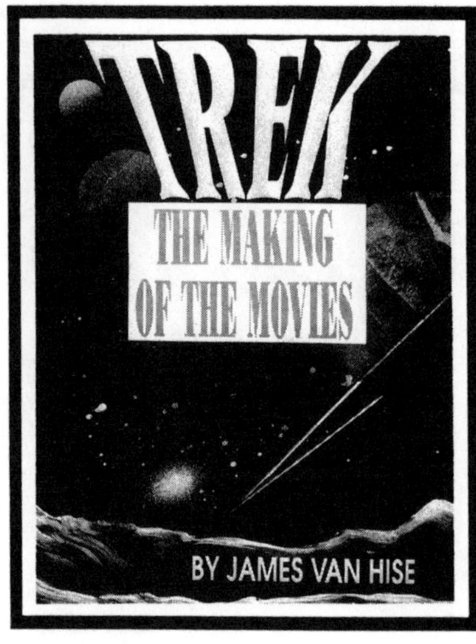

TREK: THE MAKING OF THE MOVIES

James Van Hise

TREK: THE MAKING OF THE MOVIES tells the complete story both on-screen and behind the scenes of the biggest STAR TREK adventures of all. Plus the story of the STAR TREK II that never happened and the aborted STAR TREK VI: STARFLEET ACADEMY.

$14.95.....160 Pages
ISBN # 1-55698-313-1

TREK: THE LOST YEARS

Edward Gross

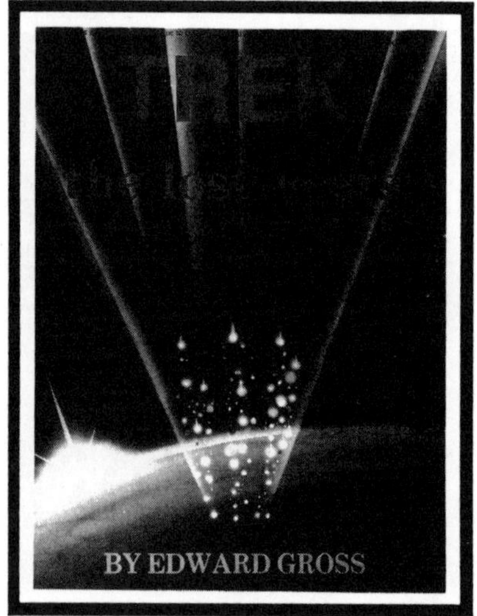

The tumultouos, behind-the-scenes saga of this modern day myth between the cancellation of the original series in 1969 and the announcement of the first movie ten years later. In addition, the text explores the scripts and treatments written throughout the 1970's, including every proposed theatrical feature and an episode guide for STAR TREK II, with comments from the writers whose efforts would ultimately never reach the screen.

This volume came together after years of research, wherein the author interviewed a wide variety of people involved with every aborted attempt at revival, from story editors to production designers to David Gautreaux, the actor signed to replace Leonard Nimoy; and had access to exclusive resource material, including memos and correspondences, as well as teleplays and script outlines.

$12.95.....132 Pages
ISBN # 1-55698-220-8

THE HISTORY OF TREK

James Van Hise

The complete story of Star Trek from Original conception to its effects on millions of Lives across the world. This book celebrates the 25th anniversary of the first "Star Trek" television episode and traces the history of the show that has become an enduring legend—even the non-Trekkies can quote specific lines and characters from the original television series. The History of Trek chronicles "Star Trek" from its start in 1966 to its cancellation in 1969; discusses the lean years when "Star Trek" wasn't shown on television but legions of die hard fans kept interest in it still alive; covers the sequence of five successful movies (and includes the upcoming sixth one); and reviews "The Next Generation" television series, now entering its sixth season. Complete with Photographs, The History of Trek reveals the origins of the first series in interviews with the original cast and creative staff. It also takes readers behind the scenes of all six Star Trek movies, offers a wealth of Star Trek Trivia, and speculates on what the future may hold.

$14.95.....160 Pages
ISBN # 1-55698-309-3

THE MAN BETWEEN THE EARS: STAR TREKS LEONARD NIMOY

James Van Hise

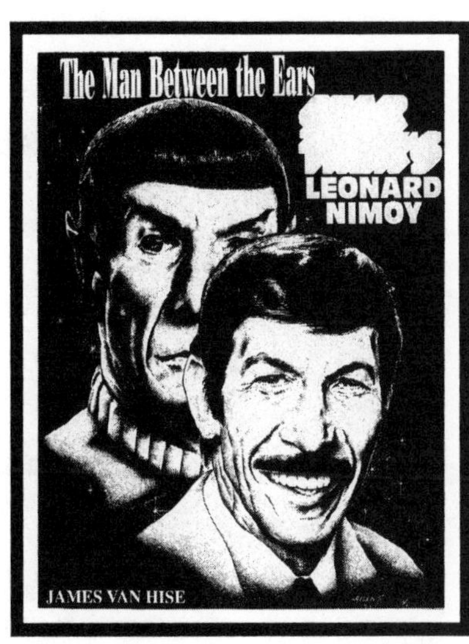

Based on his numerous interviews with Leonard Nimoy, Van Hise tells the story of the man as well as the entertainer.

This book chronicles the many talents of Leonard Nimoy from the beginning of his career in Boston to his latest starring work in the movie, Never Forget. His 25-year association with Star Trek is the centerpiece, but his work outside the Starship Enterprise is also covered, from such early efforts as Zombies of the Stratosphere to his latest directorial and acting work, and his stage debut in Vermont.

$14.95.....160 Pages
ISBN # 1-55698-304-2

THE TREK CREW BOOK

James Van Hise

The crewmembers of the starship Enterprise as presented in the original STAR TREK television series and feature film spin-offs. These fascinating characters, beloved by millions of fans, are the primary reason for the phenomenal on going success of this Gene Roddenberry created concept. Never before has a book so completely revealed this ensamble of fine actors, focusing on their careers, examining their unique portrayals of their most famous on-screen alter egos, profiling the characters themselves and presenting in-depth interviews with William Shatner, Leonard Nimoy, DeForest Kelly, James Doohan, George Takei, Walter Koenig and Nichelle Nichols.

$9.95.....108 Pages
ISBN # 1-55698-257-7

THE BEST OF ENTERPRISE INCIDENTS: THE MAGAZINE FOR STAR TREK FANS

Edited by James Van Hise

Unlike most televison series, STAR TREK inspired its millions of fans to put pen to paper in order to discuss the various themes and issues raised by the show's scripts, or to explore the nuances of the various characters, and ponder where both STAR TREK and humanity are headed in the future.

THE BEST OF THE ENTERPRISE INCIDENTS: THE MAGAZINE FOR STAR TREK FANS, is devoted entirely to such discussions, providing a collection of informative articles that have appeared over the years in ENTERPRISE INCIDENTS, the most successful STAR TREK fanzine ever published. This unique volume is written by fans for fans, and edited by the author of the TREK CREW BOOK, as well as ENTERPRISE INCIDENTS for over a decade.

$9.95.....108 Pages
ISBN # 1-55698-231-3

BORING, BUT NECESSARY ORDERING INFORMATION

Payment:

Use our new 800 # and pay with your credit card or send check or money order directly to our address. All payments must be made in U.S. funds and please do not send cash.

Shipping:

We offer several methods of shipment. Sometimes a book can be delayed if we are temporarily out of stock. You should note whether you prefer us to ship the book as soon as available, send you a merchandise credit good for other goodies, or send your money back immediately.

Normal Post Office: $3.75 for the first book and $1.50 for each additional book. These orders are filled as quickly as possible. Shipments normally take 5 to 10 days, but allow up to 12 weeks for delivery.

Special UPS 2 Day Blue Label Service or Priority Mail: Special service is available for desperate Couch Potatoes. These books are shipped within 24 hours of when we receive the order and normally take 2 to 3 three days to get to you. The cost is $10.00 for the first book and $4.00 each additional book .

Overnight Rush Service: $20.00 for the first book and $10.00 each additional book.

U.s. Priority Mail: $6.00 for the first book and $3.00.each additional book.

Canada And Mexico: $5.00 for the first book and $3.00 each additional book.

Foreign: $6.00 for the first book and $3.00 each additional book.

Please list alternatives when available and please state if you would like a refund or for us to backorder an item if it is not in stock.

ORDER FORM

_____ Trek Crew Book $9.95
_____ Best Of Enterprise Incidents $9.95
_____ Trek Fans Handbook $9.95
_____ Trek: The Next Generation $14.95
_____ The Man Who Created Star Trek: $12.95
_____ 25th Anniversary Trek Tribute $14.95
_____ History Of Trek $14.95
_____ The Man Between The Ears $14.95
_____ Trek: The Making Of The Movies $14.95
_____ Trek: The Lost Years $12.95
_____ Trek: The Unauthorized Next Generation $14.95
_____ New Trek Encyclopedia $19.95
_____ Making A Quantum Leap $14.95
_____ The Unofficial Tale Of Beauty And The Beast $14.95
_____ Complete Lost In Space $19.95
_____..doctor Who Encyclopedia: Baker $19.95
_____ Lost In Space Tribute Book $14.95
_____ Lost In Space With Irwin Allen $14.95
_____ Doctor Who: Baker Years $19.95
_____ Doctor Who: Pertwee Years $19.95
_____ Batmania Ii $14.95
_____ The Green Hornet $14.95 ____ Special Edition $16.95
_____ Number Six: The Prisoner Book $14.95
_____ Gerry Anderson: Supermarionation $17.95
_____ Addams Family Revealed $14.95
_____ Bloodsucker: Vampires At The Movies $14.95
_____ Dark Shadows Tribute $14.95
_____ Monsterland Fear Book $14.95
_____ The Films Of Elvis $14.95
_____ The Woody Allen Encyclopedia $14.95
_____ Paul Mccartney: 20 Years On His Own $9.95
_____ Yesterday: My Life With The Beatles $14.95
_____ Fab Films Of The Beatles $14.95
_____ 40 Years At Night: The Tonight Show $14.95
_____ Exposing Northern Exposure $14.95
_____ The La Lawbook $14.95
_____ Cheers: Where Everybody Knows Your Name $14.95
_____ SNL! The World Of Saturday Night Live $14.95
_____ The Rockford Phile $14.95
_____ Encyclopedia Of Cartoon Superstars $14.95
_____ How To Create Animation $14.95
_____ How To Draw Art For Comic Books $14.95
_____ King And Barker:an Illustrated Guide $14.95
_____ King And Barker: An Illustrated Guide II $14.95

100% Satisfaction Guaranteed.

We value your support. You will receive a full refund as long as the copy of the book you are not happy with is received back by us in reasonable condition. No questions asked, except we would like to know how we failed you. Refunds and credits are given as soon as we receive back the item you do not want.

NAME:_______________________

STREET:_______________________

CITY:_______________________

STATE:_______________________

ZIP:_______________________

TOTAL:________ SHIPPING________

UDS9

SEND TO: Pioneer Books, Inc. 5715 N. Balsam Rd., Las Vegas, NV 89130